DOING GOOD

DOING GOOD

Passion and Commitment
for Helping Others

Jeffrey A. Kottler, Ph.D.

BRUNNER-ROUTLEDGE
ALERE FLAMMAM
Taylor & Francis Group

USA	Publishing Office:	BRUNNER-ROUTLEDGE
		A member of the Taylor & Francis Group
		325 Chestnut Street
		Philadelphia, PA 19106
		Tel: (215) 625-8900
		Fax: (215) 625-2940
	Distribution Center:	BRUNNER-ROUTLEDGE
		A member of the Taylor & Francis Group
		7625 Empire Drive
		Florence, KY 41042
		Tel: 1-800-634-7064
		Fax: 1-800-248-4724
UK		BRUNNER-ROUTLEDGE
		A member of the Taylor & Francis Group
		27 Church Road
		Hove
		E. Sussex, BN3 2FA
		Tel: +44 (0) 1273 207411
		Fax: +44 (0) 1273 205612

DOING GOOD: Passion and Commitment for Helping Others

1 2 3 4 5 6 7 8 9 0

Printed by George H. Buchanan, Philadelphia, PA, 2000.
Cover design by Ellen Seguin. Images courtesy of Jeffrey A. Kottler.

A CIP catalog record for this book is available from the British Library.
∞ The paper in this publication meets the requirements of the ANSI Standard Z39.48-1984 (Permanence of Paper).

Library of Congress Cataloging-in-Publication Data

Kottler, Jeffrey A.
    Doing good : passion and commitment for helping others / Jeffrey A. Kottler.
      p. cm.
    Includes bibliographical references (p.) and index.
    ISBN 1-56032-887-8 (alk. paper)
    1. Altruism. 2. Helping behavior. I. Title.
  BF637.H4 K68 2000
  158′.3--dc21   00-026626

ISBN 1-56032-887-8 (paper)

CONTENTS

PREFACE

So often, books that talk about helping others focus exclusively on content, research, and skills, while ignoring the uniquely human dimensions that are involved in this endeavor. Certainly there is a systematic research and knowledge base to the helping professions, as well as a set of generic skills and interventions, but there is also a degree of passion and commitment associated with doing good for others. Whether you are a student in counseling, psychology, social work, family therapy, education, nursing, or other human services; a professional practitioner of these disciplines; or a volunteer working in local, regional, national, or international agencies, this book is intended to inspire you to make a difference in your work with others.

Told through the experiences of those who "do good" for a living or as an avocation, this book reflects the realities of helping others among those who are successful and flourishing in their work. Unlike more traditional texts that concentrate solely on theory or techniques, this work is focused on helping beginners to feel good about their commitment to service. It is thus appropriate as a text in both undergraduate and graduate courses such as Introduction to Counseling, Introduction to Human Services, Social Work I, Introduction to Education, Nursing Practice, and similar survey courses. It will be equally useful to both professionals and those involved in volunteer helping efforts within community, religious, and state organizations.

☐ Overview

The book's organization flows from a brief, but more general and scholarly discussion of the subject, to one that is distinctly more personal. It is the voices of counselors, therapists, nurses, physicians, philanthropists, teachers, public service personnel, and volunteers who give this book life. It is through their eyes and hearts that you will enter the world of doing good.

In the first chapter, you will look at what it means to help others for a living or an avocation, exploring some of the joys of this work, as well as the special challenges. It is often difficult to know, for instance, when and if you do make a difference in someone's life and whether the effects will last.

Chapter 2 examines some of the theories and research that explain altruism, integrating what is known to account for this very complex behavior that has mystified so many social scientists. You will learn about the evolutionary basis for how altruism evolved, as well as the roles of justice, empathy, social responsibility, and compassion.

The third chapter introduces the voices of a dozen helpers who explain their own motives for why they have devoted their lives to service and what they get out of this commitment. Chapter 4 continues the discussion, but with a very different slant: The focus is on the very personal benefits that accrue to those who help others.

Chapter 5 distills the very complex process of helping into its essential components. Practitioners talk about what they believe they do that makes the most difference in people's lives. From their narratives a summary is presented of what matters most in attempts to do good.

While the focus of this book is primarily on the passion, exhilaration, and excitement that accompany acts of service, there are also some sacrifices that are made along the way. In Chapter 6, helpers talk about the price they pay for their devotion and commitment. The following chapter also examines some of the obstacles that must be overcome during the helping process, as well as excuses that are often used by helpers to avoid doing so much more.

The final chapter provides you with practical advice about where to go next in your efforts to make yourself the most powerful, effective, and caring helper that you can be.

ACKNOWLEDGMENTS

I would like to express my deep appreciation to a number of altruistic helpers who were willing to talk about their service to others, the price they pay for this commitment, and the joy they feel as a result of their efforts. While many individuals prefer to go unnamed, the following professionals and volunteers agreed to share their experiences: Bill Anderson, Fred Bemak, Diane Blau, Peter Bowman, Christine Breier, Jon Carlson, Laurie Carty, Mei-Whei Chen, Elizabeth Dole, Rosemary Forrest, Deborah Fraser, Anne Geroski, Richard Hazler, Paul Jones, Jeanne Lightly, Sandy Magnuson, Aretha Marbley, Georgene McReynolds, Gerald Monk, Jerry Parr, Mary Spaeth, Guðbjörg Vilhjálmsdóttir, and Sherrill Wiseman.

Finally, I wish to thank Tim Julet, Acquisitions Editor at Brunner-Routledge, for his thoughtful and constructive input, turning the idea behind this book into a tangible product.

Jeffrey A. Kottler
Las Vegas, Nevada
May 2000

Welcome With Open Arms

I have been studying altruism throughout most of my life, trying to figure out why some people give of themselves to others, even when it involves a great investment of time, energy, and commitment. There appears to be no apparent gain for the one who is doing good, other than some elusive feeling of well-being, a kind of "helper's high."

The idea for the systematic study of this subject began for me some time ago while I was walking down the street and I came upon a child in trouble. This little boy was sitting on the sidewalk, his knapsack turned upside down and his papers scattered across the street like snowflakes. Tears were streaming down his face as an older, bigger girl taunted him. Finally, his nemesis boarded a school bus, leaving the little boy to suffer alone.

It was at this moment that I came upon the scene. I reached down, collected the child's things, gathered them together in a neat pile, and then helped him up. At first timid, suspicious, and reticent, he eventually gave me the most glorious smile I have ever seen. Here was this human being in pain and because I was walking down the street at an opportune moment, I was positioned to offer some help, to make a difference in some small way in this person's life.

Never in my life have I felt more useful. This child's smile washed over me, soothed me. I felt giddy. I could no longer remember where I was

A part of this chapter was adapted from a previous article by the author: Doing Good: Counseling and the Helper's High. *Journal of Humanistic Education and Development,* 33, 94–96, 1994. Reprinted with permission by the American Counseling Association.

headed or what was so important that I had to rush along. I waited with this child until the next bus came along, and I felt that, somehow, my whole day was justified. I could sleep well that night feeling like I had done something worthwhile. This was such an insignificant act, reaching out to a stranger, yet it embodied everything wonderful to me about the practice of helping. Feeling useful, doing good, are the reasons why most of us entered the helping professions in the first place (Guy, Poelstra, & Stark, 1987).

☐ What's Missing in Professional and Volunteer Training

When you review the curricular plan for your training, you will notice that considerable effort has gone into developing a sequential flow of courses that equip you with the theory, research, and methodologies you will need in your work. You will read lots of books, take tests, write papers, practice skills, discuss ideas, observe helping encounters, and apply what you have learned to actual situations. All of this background is extremely valuable in your professional growth and development.

When people who have been helped talk about what made the greatest difference to them, they don't necessarily mention the same things that their helpers thought were most important. Sometimes, they report on how supported and validated they felt. They like the kind of relationship that provides a structure for making needed changes, but one that is caring and safe. And they appreciate professionals who demonstrate certain personal qualities like confidence, genuineness, compassion, flexibility, sensitivity, and emotional receptiveness (Jennings & Skovholt, 1999; Kottler, 1991; Miller, 1993).

In spite of what people say they want most in someone who offers aid, as a student you will not necessarily receive much attention toward developing those personal qualities that will make you more charismatic, sensitive, and influential. One reason may be that people don't always know what is best for themselves; otherwise, it is the patients who would do the diagnosis and treatment planning when they visit their doctors. Imagine going to see a physician because you have a headache, suggesting to her that you think you have a brain tumor, and then scheduling your own operation to remove it.

Second, there is relatively little attention directed towards acts of generosity and altruism. Oh, we occasionally put a hero or two on a pedestal, celebrate someone who does something extraordinarily generous, or pin a medal on a civilian or soldier who risks his or her life. However, compared to the media attention directed toward acts of evil—serial murder, mass carnage, terrorism, war, genocide, atrocities, torture—human generosity receives scant space. Brehony (1999) wonders why there is such a human fascination and public interest in evil over goodness. In her book compiling accounts of compassion and kindness, she laments the obsession with depravity and horror: "Made aware of so much evil, we have become numbed by it. Many of us are no longer outraged or even surprised by heinous acts" (p. 4).

It seems to be assumed that we are born either good or evil and there is no sense messing with human nature. But we all have within us the capacity for being both selfish and generous, vindictive and forgiving, sinners or saints. In the most supportive environments each of us can be encouraged to access that part of us that is most compassionate and caring.

A third reason why relatively little time and effort is devoted to developing altruism, caring, and compassion is because they are qualities so difficult to define, measure, and teach. It is assumed that you've got them or you don't. Even if that assumption was true (which it is probably not), we don't do very much to select prospective professionals who already have these attributes. In fact, we go to the other extreme, choosing students who are bright, ambitious, high achievers, good writers and test takers, none of which are necessarily associated with doing good for others. Students are chosen based on being driven rather than caring, compulsively achieving rather than flexible, smart rather than sensitive.

Sarason (1995) has voiced the concern that training programs in medicine, law, and psychology in particular do not prepare their practitioners to be caring and compassionate in their work. In the fields of education, social work, counseling, family therapy, and human services, professionals are heavily dosed with theory, research, and intervention methodologies while personal qualities are all but ignored. It is as if a doctor, nurse, teacher, lawyer, or therapist must merely master the technology of the discipline in order to be helpful. Lost in this mentality are the powers of the healing relationship and other human dimensions.

Sarason (1995) listed a number of examples to support his thesis that caring and compassion are not particularly valued by helping professions and their training programs. Just look at the way that doctors, lawyers, and psychologists, for instance, are prepared. They are subjected to incredible pressure, sleep deprivation, cut-throat competition, and inhuman schedules. They live in constant fear of being evaluated and found wanting. It isn't safe to express what you really think, to be genuine and authentic, or you will get eaten alive. And the emphasis throughout the curriculum is on content (filling the professional up with stuff) rather than process (relationship, interactive, and human dimensions).

Repeatedly, trainees are admonished not to get too involved with those they are helping: "Keep your distance." "Don't care too much." This is, of course, good advice. It is a good thing to protect yourself from overinvolvement in cases, to avoid countertransference issues, and to maintain appropriate boundaries so that you don't burn out. Unfortunately, this position is taken to such an extreme that being caring and compassionate is sometimes associated with losing control.

I interviewed a doctor who told me that, especially for a woman, it is death to be caught crying on the job. Physicians are taught to be dispassionate, objective, detached, scientific—to only rarely show their human side. "Medical school destroyed whatever soft part of me I held dear," she said with real sadness. "In order to succeed, more than that, in order to excel as one of the few women around, I had to act like a man" (Kottler, 1996b, p. 135). Of course, what she really meant is that she was supposed to hide her caring towards patients. This physician described what happened once when she visited a cancer patient who needed her vital signs checked. "After I took her blood pressure, I kept her hand in mine and we just cried together. It was so moving—until the resident burst in and demanded to know what the hell was going on: 'And you want to be a doctor?' he said sarcastically. 'If you are going to pull shit like this, why don't you just be a nurse!' "

If only this was a rare event. Alas, it is not, especially in male-dominated cultures like the worlds of business, medicine, and law. At least in education, psychology, social work, nursing, counseling, and human services, which are dominated instead by more female-oriented values, we do have greater permission to access and express our genuine feelings—that is, if we work in environments that permit such displays. All too often, this is not the case. By appearing too caring, loving, and helpful, you risk being perceived as a "lightweight," an idealistic do-gooder who doesn't see reality.

The reality is that we are besieged by paperwork, administrative chores, and endless meetings. More than ever, dwindling resources and the managed care movement have forced us to value efficiency, billable hours, and head counts over anything else we do. One school counselor shakes her head in wonderment when she considers the difference between what she learned in school and what she does in her job.

"Don't get me wrong," she is quick to point out, concerned with the tendency to blame others for our own unpreparedness. "I had some good professors and some good classes. I learned lots of cool stuff about counseling. The thing is, I can't remember the last time I used any of it."

She smiles at that last comment, but we both know she isn't really kidding. "Oh yeah," she remembers, "a couple of days ago I had a kid come in who was upset about his schedule or something. I just pounced on him and made him sit down and talk to me. He was more than willing to oblige but he couldn't figure out what I was doing: He only wanted his schedule changed. What I wanted was to really help someone using the skills I learned in school.

"Here I am, supposedly this expert counselor, and all I really am is a glorified secretary. They could teach a few work-study students to do what I do. Look at this [she points around her office]. I've got not only one computer but two of them to process all the paper work I do."

Many professionals have all but given up trying to beat a system that measures productivity as the number of cases processed, the number of files closed, or the amount of fees one generates. Indeed, there is an incredible amount of paperwork associated with the job. Yet there are lots and lots of professionals who find a way to work within the system and still maintain the highest standards of personal integrity, honor, and compassion.

One such individual works as a case worker investigating accusations of child abuse. "You just can't believe all the stuff they make me do," she explains with exasperation. "I'm not actually a state employee but a subcontractor, so I have even more paperwork to deal with. They keep me on this status so they don't have to pay benefits and all. I don't care, though, 'cause I'm never in an office.

"I see people at their worst. They are either trying to hide something from me so they're lying through their teeth, or they have been falsely accused and they are angry. Sometimes it's real hard to tell the difference.

"I used to think there wasn't a lot I could do to help these people. My employer defines my job as trying to get at the truth, which really means to find out if the parents should be charged or not. But I think that the best thing I do is try to be as kind a listener as I can. That way they not only tell me more, but it feels to them as if the system isn't impersonal, that there really is someone who cares. After all, to them I *am* the system."

That's lesson number 1 about the job of doing good. Regardless of the system in which you operate, the petty bureaucratic regulations you must live under, the pressure you feel to demonstrate efficiency and productivity, even the ingratitude you will sometimes feel from your clients, you must demonstrate consistently that you genuinely care about what you are doing and the people you are helping. That might sound pretty easy for a newcomer to the field filled with a spirit of optimism and enthusiasm. But look around you at all the veterans who once felt like you do. Now so many of them are dispirited and cynical. Ask yourself what happened to them along the line. At one time they were just like you.

☐ Knowing You Have Made a Difference

I have spoken at length (Kottler, 1993, 1996a, 1998; Kottler & Hazler, 1997; Kottler & Zehm, 2000) about the privilege and honor that results from being a helper, sanctioned by society to make a difference in people's lives. People come to us in excruciating pain or with a hunger to learn. They look to us for salvation, to guide them out of the abyss of hopelessness, to provide enlightenment. Yet, during this journey we take together, the client is certainly not the only one who profits from the experience. There are times when we learn about ourselves as much as our clients grow from the interactions. There is also that mysterious, magical feeling of exhilaration when we know that as a result of our efforts somebody's life is somehow enriched.

Even with all the strains and stresses of helping work, the burdens of responsibility, the uncertainty and doubts, there are few joys greater than knowing that we have been helpful to someone. That is one reason why 100 million adults in the United States alone do some type of volunteer service, spending an average of 4 hours per week taking care of needy people (Independent Sector, 1996).

We all plug along, doing our best to be helpful. Many times we are not altogether certain that our efforts are successful, or even appreciated. But there are those all-too-rare occasions when we are absolutely positive that we have done some good.

☐ Can We Really Know the Good We Do?

I have been speaking as if it is obvious when you have helped someone, that you know that you have done good. Yet it is one of the realities of this work that you often don't know who you have really helped and who you have not. People lie. What they report to us isn't necessarily what happened. They even deceive themselves as well, whispering that they have become transformed when they still engage in the same self-defeating behaviors. Just as frustrating: They may refuse to admit to us, or anyone else, that they are any different when it seems pretty obvious that things are no longer the same.

Let's assume that you wish to help others because it feels good to know that you have made some sort of difference. If that's the case, you have a bit of a problem. One therapist in private practice talks about her strong belief that we are never accurate judges of the differences we make.

"Until I told them, the people who made heart-touching, life-changing differences in my own life never were aware of this and were, in fact, shocked at the news. They were even a little embarrassed. I suppose on some level I selected those people to help me for precisely that reason. Had they been focused on their own difference-making and been arrogant enough to think that they had the power to save me, I would have quickly picked up on their card-carrying, self-proclaimed membership in DSS—the Department of Savior Services."

This therapist cracks me up—her way with words—and yet just like those who have helped her most without realizing it, she is deaf to her own eloquence. With a little prodding, she continues her observations about being unaware of the good we do.

"The other day I was waiting at a stoplight and the minivan in front of me had a fairly small rectangular opening in the back end. There was a sticker beside it which contained an arrow pointing to the nonvisible contents inside the hole, noting 'hidden hitch'. When I saw this I laughed.

"The people who have been the greatest helpers in my own life had this sticker glued across their backs, although they were unable to see this sign. It reminds me when I unknowingly walked around in my third grade classroom with a taped-on sign across my backend that said, 'kick me'. These dynamic helpers have this subtly taped-on sign indicating 'hidden hitch'. They are *connectable*. They have hidden hitches all over their being."

Think about this idea for a moment. If what this therapist says is really true, that we can never really grasp the good we do, that such changes are invisible to us, that the differences we think we make are delusional, that the people we think we failed we really might have helped a lot . . . Enough! This gives me a headache.

While I accept that we can't be *perfectly* accurate judges of our impact on others, surely with experience and training, we become skilled at assessing reasonably clearly which outcomes have resulted from our efforts. If this is not the case, it is hard to imagine that we can be very consistent and potent in our helping. After all, the very act of doing good for others involves reading accurately what we believe is needed; implementing the preferred intervention for that person, in that situation, with those specific complaints; and then observing very carefully what results from these efforts. If there does not *appear* to be a good outcome, then we try something else.

Nevertheless, I think what this therapist is reminding us about is our own humility. There are so many people who do good primarily to feed their egos and inflate their own sense of power. They like holding others' lives in their hands. They enjoy the control that comes with this type of work, in which they are the ones in charge. They thrive on the approval and gratitude they get from others and use the compliments to prop up their fragile egos.

In welcoming you to this field of helping, I would be remiss if I didn't warn you that there are temptations to take yourself very seriously, to feel pompous and self-important. The therapist who just spoke earlier is very uncomfortable admitting, much less ever talking about the fact, that she does this work because it feels good.

"If I am ever thanked for the help I give others, I don't know what I feel. I go through this battery of self-assessment on the spot. Am I feeling good while receiving this praise? Am I feeling ashamed that if I was *truly* great, I wouldn't be savoring this moment and sucking up the compliments as much as I am? Is there some way I can bask in this glory and not show it?"

She pauses for a moment, as if replaying what she just said to see if it makes sense.

"Anyway," she continues, "Who is actually responsible for the help? Did the person do it on his own? Did I foster dependency or meet my own need for approval? Am I the one who really made the difference? Did I even have a part at all? And am I supposed to play a role in this process but not admit it?"

She nods her head, more certain of herself and where she is going with this.

"If I was really great, would I think so? Did Ghandi or Mother Teresa think they were so special?"

She stops here, stunned for the moment, realizing she has revealed far more than she ever intended. She feels vulnerable and transparent.

"Oops," she says with a nervous smile.

So many questions to think about in the act of helping. It is so difficult and disorienting to consider the impact of what you are doing, whether you can ever really know what you have done. Just as confusing is trying to sort out why you are really doing good for others, as well as what you are trying to do for yourself along the way.

You will be relieved to know that most helpers aren't quite as hard on themselves as this woman. It is not actually *required* that you doubt yourself and question almost everything you do. It does help, however, to maintain a certain degree of caution, and yes, humility, regarding your role in this often mysterious process of change.

☐ What Qualifies as Doing Good?

Before we examine further the consequences of altruism and service, it is important that we be clear about what qualifies as such an effort. For example, is it considered altruistic if you help someone but with a hidden motive to get something in return? Here is a more difficult question: What if you extend yourself to someone, say, volunteer to help with a worthy project, but as a result you get favorable publicity that increases your stature in others' eyes?

There are actually several different kinds of "prosocial behavior," all of which involve acts beneficial to others (Schroeder, Penner, Dovidio, & Pili-avin, 1995). *Helping* involves doing something that improves the well-being of another. This can involve anything from providing aid during an emergency to the most casual act of lending a tool to a neighbor. *Altruism* is a particular kind of helping without anticipation of any reward or reciprocal benefit. A more strict definition would include some form of self-sacrifice on the helper's part. Motivation is also a key factor in that the *intention* was not for personal gain. Third, *cooperation* involves the sort of help with mutual benefit; there is an agreed-upon exchange of services.

The various nuances of what qualifies as altruistic behavior have been classified into three main varieties (Galston, 1993). *Personal altruism* represents acts of generosity that are directed solely towards those with whom one enjoys an affiliative relationship, namely, friends and family. *Communal altruism* is broadened a bit more to include doing good for those who are members of your identified community or ethnic, religious, or community group. Finally, *cosmopolitan altruism* involves acts of self-sacrifice that are directed to the human race as a whole, without regard for special interests or ties.

For our purposes, we are addressing mostly the communal and cosmopolitan variants, those that involve selfless acts towards relative strangers rather than kin. Let's be even more precise about this subject. A truly altruistic act meets the following conditions (Monroe, 1996):

1. It must involve action, rather than mere thought. It is not sufficient to plan something nice for someone, to consider doing something good, unless you actually follow through on your resolve.
2. Intention is more important than results. Regardless of how things turn out, whether you are able to be effective or not in your efforts, it is the thought that counts (as long as you act on that thought).
3. The primary goal of the act must be to help someone else, rather than yourself. Personal gains must be unintended, or at least secondary.
4. There is some personal sacrifice or risk involved. By definition, altruism must cost you something in terms of time, effort, resources, position, safety, or health.
5. There are no strings attached, no expectations for reward or reciprocal benefits.

You can see now that a truly altruistic gesture is not without its price. I would add to the above criteria another factor that applies to paid professionals who receive compensation for teaching, writing, or counseling. You can be fairly rewarded for your time and still engage in worthwhile, relatively selfless acts of giving. The key ingredient is whether what you are doing is for extrinsic rewards (money, fame, power) or to truly make a difference (to complicate matters, the motives are often mixed). Remember, as with most moral choices, the intention matters more than results.

☐ Acting on What You Know

Doing a traditional literature search in the library, you would find that there is little immediately accessible material on the subject of altruism and doing good. Historically, several early writers in the field, even going back to Greek philosophers, talk about the personal obligation every citizen has to promote the welfare of their culture. In modern times, Adler (1979) advocated the concept of "social interest" as part of his theory. While he envisioned this as similar to empathy—"to see with the eyes of another, to hear with the ears of another, to feel with the heart of another" (Adler, 1956, p. 135)—it also encompassed a sense of communal responsibility and proactive encouragement (Watts, 1999).

Although other theoreticians such as Carl Rogers and Virginia Satir also devoted a significant part of their lives to advocating on behalf of social issues like world peace, poverty, and selfless acts of service, most attention in our field is directed primarily toward helping our own clients, which is certainly enough work to keep us busy for several lifetimes.

There is a body of research on the phenomenon of the "helper's high." In *How Can I Help?*, Ram Das and Gorman (1985) collected a series of first-person accounts of what it means to be a helper. There are case examples of a nurse working on a neonatal intensive care unit who holds critically ill infants in her arms so they do not die alone; of a clown who comforts seriously burned children by drying their tears of pain with popcorn and then eating their tears. There are poignant and yet very familiar portraits of what it means to be a helper and of the emotional consequences, both positive and negative, of reaching out to others.

Luks (1988) described the psychophysiological research that has been done on the phenomenon of the "helper's high," in which certain hormonal and neurological changes take place during altruistic acts. There is indeed evidence for the prevalence of a "helper's high," and a number of research studies have been done on the neural mechanisms that predispose us to act altruistically, and subsequently be rewarded by our endocrine systems with a feeling of well-being (see Hunt [1990] for a highly readable review of the subject).

Glantz and Pearce (1989) and Dugatkin (1999) described how sociobiologists have been trying to explain for years why it is that if the purpose of life is to perpetuate our own gene pool, why is it that we will give of ourselves when it is not in our own best interests? How do we explain the conduct of a person who rescues a stranger knowing that he or she will forfeit his or her own life in the process? A starling will sacrifice itself to save its brethren from a hawk because it has been genetically programmed to do so. But for us, such a selfless act is a matter of choice.

The problem is not really a dearth of research and writing to consult on the subject. There are many biographies that describe the lives of people who have devoted themselves to the service of others. There are great novels whose characters inspire us through their courage in reaching out to others. There is an increasing body of qualitative literature in which investigators are attempting to describe more fully the experience of helping others.

The challenge is not in finding enough to read, it is in acting on what we know. With the choice you have made to be a helper, the important thing to consider is what you have done to make a difference. How have you extended yourself, not as part of your work, but as part of your humaneness, to reach out to someone? The question that I am most committed to considering as I lie in bed at night, waiting for sleep to overtake me is: What good have I done today?

As you lie in your own bed tonight, as you reflect on your day, what can you say about what you did that matters?

☐ More Than a Job

In this book you will have the opportunity to reflect on your motives for choosing a life devoted to helping others. You will explore your personal needs and values, investigate your deepest convictions, and clarify what it is that you hope to do and how you wish to do it. In other books and other courses, you will master the basic research, theory, and technology of the helping professions. You will examine such questions as why people choose to help others and what they get out of this commitment; what the benefits and sacrifices are of being a helper; how you can make the greatest impact on others while still taking care of yourself; how you can overcome the obstacles that you will face along your professional journey.

I am certain that you already realize that this work of doing good for others is far more than a job. In an interview with former head of the Red Cross and former Presidential candidate, Elizabeth Dole, she talked about the moment she finally realized why she had been devoting so much of her time and energy to the mission of her organization. Flying home from a relief and rescue mission in Kuwait, she realized she had never felt more fulfilled.

"I've stood by the side of my Red Cross staff in Florida," Dole says with real feeling at the memory, "as we braced for Hurricane Andrew. I've cradled a gaunt Rwandan baby in my arms. And I've sat with our men and women in uniform, far from home and loved ones, as they kept the peace in Bosnia. I have seen things that will haunt me the rest of my life. But I've been able to make a difference for people with dire human needs. This has been more than a job to me."

As Dole reminisces about a life devoted to service, she would probably have to acknowledge that personal ambition plays a part, as it does for most of us. But if the goal is to become rich or famous, or even to receive lots of approval, you are in the wrong place. This work is far more than a job; it *is* a calling that requires almost limitless devotion and energy.

I welcome you with open arms to the professions devoted to doing good. May your own passion and commitment sustain you, just as you hope to make others' lives more satisfying and fulfilling.

2

Why Do People Help Others and What Do They Get Out of It?

There are so many reasons why people choose to help others, some to address personal needs, others to meet altruistic or moral imperatives. For most of us, it is a combination of factors that led (or pushed) us to a life devoted to service.

"Giving, like love, is an element of both charity and philanthropy," writes Bremner (1994, p. xi) in his history of the subject. "Love sometimes is left out, but giving is essential." People give out of love, but for other reasons as well: habit, obligation, brownie points to get into heaven, social approval, tax deductions, peer pressure, guilt, friendship, or business opportunities.

A number of scholars and writers have explored the subject of altruism, trying to uncover the mysteries of why someone would deliberately and intentionally engage in behavior to help someone when there are considerable risks of personal sacrifice. Charles Darwin (1859) first struggled with this dilemma when he formulated his theory of evolution. He found it difficult to reconcile the kind of selfish behavior that preserves one's own chances for survival with putting oneself at deliberate risk for the sake of others. At one point, he believed his whole theory was in jeopardy unless he could unravel this "irrational" behavior.

When E. O. Wilson (1975) adapted evolutionary theory to examine social behavior, he also wrestled with the phenomenon of altruism as the ultimate theoretical challenge, preferring to stay away from humans as much as possible. Since that time, quite a number of scholars and writers have tackled the subject of altruism, including evolutionary psychologists (Sober

& Wilson, 1998), sociologists (Jeffries, 1998), social psychologists (Batson, 1986; Rushton, 1976), developmental psychologists (Eisenberg, 1982; Zahn-Waxler, 1983), organizational psychologists (Korsgaard, Beglino, & Lester, 1997), evolutionary biologists (Dugatkin, 1999; Trivers, 1971), science writers (Hunt, 1990; Kohn, 1990; Wright, 1994), and philosophers (Singer, 1981).

What most of these researchers conclude is that altruism is only part of what drives people to do good for others. Furthermore, the motives of philanthropists are often very different from that of rescuers or heroines (Monroe, 1996). Nevertheless, a certain amount of generosity and giving does turn out to be evolutionarily functional, if not for the individual, then certainly for the larger community. We are all connected to one another through our shared genetic material, argues cellular biologist Lewis Thomas (1983); we all originated from the same ancestral cell. "We have an enormous family to look after," he says. We must "acknowledge these family ties," he urges further, "and with them, the obligations" (pp. 106–107).

☐ Why Being Generous Is Better Than Being Selfish, Evolutionarily Speaking

If you know the least bit about evolutionary theory, then you know that among plants and animals most developments and behavior are intended to be adaptive. In other words, life is organized around the premise that organisms do what they must in order to survive or, better yet, insure that their offspring survive so that a part of them will live on. This is the only measure of success, biologically speaking.

While this explanation certainly has its critics, you must surely agree that among members of our species, there is compelling evidence that people (and other organisms) tend to do what is in their self-interest. This may sound unduly cynical, especially in a book about the altruistic spirit of doing good for others, but human beings are inclined to weigh their actions against one overriding question: What's in it for me? If some investment of your time and energy does not result in a measurable personal gain, why on earth would you extend yourself in that way? Why would you make personal sacrifices, risk your life, waste resources or energy, if such actions do not increase the likelihood of your own survival and that of others who share your genetic material?

These are questions that are far more difficult to answer than you might imagine. How do you explain, for example, why someone would sacrifice his or her life to save a perfect stranger? Perhaps it is comprehensible that a soldier would take a bullet or fall on a grenade to save his buddies. It certainly is not at all unusual that someone would die to save her family.

But there are also numerous cases of individuals who have knowingly given up their lives so that others—people they have never even met—can live.

If risking one's life is an extreme example of self-sacrifice, there are many others that are just as puzzling. If it is true that our "job" in life is to make sure that we leave behind a legacy of our genes, then why do some people choose not to have children? And why would any of us willingly select a path in life that involves devoting our lives to serving others without apparent material gain? Evolutionary theorists have answers to these questions but they are not altogether convincing. The reality is that doing good is one of the wonderful mysteries of the human universe.

At first (or second) glance, it seems rather obvious that individuals who help others at cost to themselves will have fewer offspring than those who are selfish. If you give away your time, effort, and energy to serve others without receiving some reciprocal benefit, then you have squandered resources that could have been devoted to your own genetic offspring and kin. That is not exactly the sort of behavior that is adaptive and would therefore not be selected to evolve over time. But that's only if we look at the small picture.

A number of theorists have attempted to apply Darwinian notions of survival-based drives to explain human behavior. Beginning with Edmund Wilson's (1975, 1979) groundbreaking work in sociobiology and evolutionary psychology and continuing with other applications to the fields of mental health and morality (see Breuer, 1982; Glantz & Pearce, 1989; Singer, 1981; Wenegrat, 1984 as examples), there has been a concerted effort to apply evolutionary, genetics-based programming to account for human behavior. These theories have not been without their critics who claim that this approach is unduly deterministic, even racist, because of its' emphasis on the biological basis for actions.

Among the challenges that these theorists have faced is trying to make sense of why people do engage in behavior that appears to be less than self-serving and that decreases the likelihood of survival and procreation. Recently, several writers (Dugatkin, 1999; Hunt, 1990; Sober & Wilson, 1998; Wright, 1994) have discussed this issue, concluding in part that altruism can be adaptive as well, if not for the individual, then certainly for the larger community. After all, even if evolutionary theorists are right that much of behavior is designed to help us survive, the operative word there is "us." Not only are we driven to protect ourselves, but also to make sure that our community remains stable and healthy. Without an intact support system, our relatives and friends would be left without defenses.

"An altruist may have fewer offspring than a nonaltruist within its own group," Sober and Wilson (1998) admit, "but groups of altruists will have more offspring than groups of nonaltruists" (p. 4). In other words, being selfish might help a single individual to increase the likelihood of personal survival, and that of his or her offspring, but at the expense of community functioning. Those cultures and tribes that exhibit an altruistic spirit are going to function in more efficient ways and therefore produce more children who are likely to survive longer. That is why altruists are often so valued, honored, and protected by their societies: They increase the likelihood that the community, as a whole, will be more effectively competitive in the process of natural selection (Monroe, 1996).

☐ Why Animals and Humans Do Good

Numerous examples are supplied of altruistic phenomena in the animal kingdom in which individuals have put themselves on the line to protect and serve others. Some of the most compelling illustrations are listed below.

1. Robins, thrushes, and other birds will sound warnings when predators arrive on the scene, drawing attention to themselves in order to allow their fellows to escape (Trivers, 1971).
2. A squirrel will screech out an alarm at the sight of a hawk, allowing others to find safe shelter at the personal cost of making itself a target (Sherman, 1980).
3. Bees will launch kamikaze-like attacks against intruders to save their hive even though their heroic acts result in certain death. Termites, ants, and other social insects have developed a whole caste system of citizens whose sole job it is to sacrifice themselves on behalf of others (Thomas, 1983).
4. Among Sonoran Desert ants, only one citizen, the queen, goes out to forage and gather food for everyone else in the colony. Furthermore, among the queens available, one actually volunteers for the duty rather than being subjected to it through coercion (Rissing, Pollock, Higgins, Hagen, & Smith, 1989).
5. Certain monkeys and other apes will distract a lion or other predator in the vicinity so the rest of the troop can escape, knowing that they will most certainly be eaten instead (Gould & Marler, 1987).
6. When chimpanzees of one troop have found a good food source, say a fruit rich tree, they will make sufficient noise to attract others, even though this will mean less for themselves (Singer, 1981).
7. Among wolves, one adult member of the pack will choose to forgo "marriage" and its own territory in order to help the alpha male and female raise their own brood (Masson & McCarthy, 1995).

As impressed as you might be by these selfless acts, human beings are even more remarkable because we make a conscious choice to be altruistic rather than operating solely from instinct (Hunt, 1990). Some of the best explanations to account for this sacrificial, altruistic behavior in humans and other animals are postulated by Dugatkin (1999) to include kinship bonds, reciprocal altruism, and cost–benefit analysis.

Kinship Bonds

The geneticist J. B. S. Haldane (1955) is widely credited with observing that he would risk his life to save two siblings or eight cousins. What he meant by this is that the amount of genetic material he shares with two siblings or eight first cousins works out to be mathematically equivalent to his own evolutionary worth. This is the simplest and most commonsense explanation for altruistic behavior: that people will risk their lives or make sacrifices if it is for the benefit of their kin. Likewise, acts of aggression and sabotage would be far more likely to occur with nonrelatives (Ashton, Paunonen, Helmes, & Jackson, 1998).

One of the more intriguing studies to substantiate that theory is the observation that male lions routinely kill the children of vanquished males or of new mates, so that they do not invest any time feeding or caring for creatures that are not of their making (Bluffer-Hrdy, 1976). If that isn't disturbing enough, consider that humans do the same thing, at least symbolically speaking, since the incidence of child abuse is 100 times greater when a step-parent is present in the home (Daly & Wilson, 1988; Buss, 1999).

Evolutionary advantages are only part of the picture in behaving altruistically for the benefit of blood relatives. In one study of kidney transplant donors, the donors almost invariably reported that their acts of generosity, at great personal risk, were among the most important things they had ever done in their lives (Fellner & Marshall, 1981). Even when the kidneys were rejected, meaning that the altruistic act was in vain, the donors still had no regrets.

It is not surprising that we devote time and energy to serve people who are members of our kinship group, whether that includes immediate or extended family or even "tribal affiliations" like neighborhoods, religions, churches, and professional guilds. Even though this sounds particularly cynical, there is a kind of self-interest involved when you extend yourself to help others who share your genes, or at least your mutual interests. When members of your neighborhood, church, team, or "clan" do well, such benefits reflect favorably on you as well.

Reciprocal Altruism

I had just met the 12 strangers who would be part of my Sierra Club backpacking trip along the coast of Northern California. We had just gone through basic introductions, but I am horrible at remembering names, so they were all running together in my head.

"Damn," I could hear one guy mumble to himself. "Damn. Damn. Damn."

"Forget something?" I asked politely, trying to remember his name.

"Yeah," he said with some exasperation. "I always forget something important on these trips. This time it's the leash that holds my sunglasses."

Before I could stop myself, before I could even think about what I was doing, I heard myself say to him, "Here, take mine. I don't really like using one anyway."

"Are you sure?" he asked me cautiously. He seemed dumbfounded that a perfect stranger would give him just what he needed most.

"Yeah, no problem." Then embarrassed by my own generosity, I offered an excuse. "I don't really like these things anyway so I wouldn't even use it."

What had come over me, I wondered? Was this truly a selfless act without any concern for compensation or a reciprocal favor?

I promise you that at the time I didn't give the slightest conscious thought to anything else except that here was a person who needed something that I was in a position to offer. It just felt good to step in and be of assistance. Period.

The story doesn't end here, however. A few days later, this man was the designated cook for the evening's meal. We were all starving after having walked a good many miles up and down mountainsides carrying our heavy packs. When it was my turn through the food line, the guy gave me this huge portion of food, probably double what anyone else received. I looked up at him and he winked.

Without ever talking about it directly, it was understood between us, or certainly in his mind, that he owed me something for my earlier generosity. This wasn't part of any bargain of which I was aware; I expected nothing from this guy. If anything, I was uncomfortable that he felt he owed me some sort of debt. Sure enough, throughout the rest of the week-long trip, he continually found ways to repay my favor—saving me choice ground for my tent, helping me on with my pack, encouraging me during one climb when I was dragging. We ended up fast friends, all because of one thoughtless gesture.

This typical human interaction is known as "I'll scratch your back, you scratch mine." According to this explanation, people will extend themselves to help others who are not kin if they believe, unconsciously or consciously, that this effort will result in some reciprocal favor. People happen to have remarkable memories when it comes to remembering gestures—who owes you and who you are indebted to (especially the former). We are natural scorekeepers, Dugatkin (1999) says; Natural selection has developed this capacity in us so that we can be sure to collect on our debts.

Before you protest, supplying many examples of situations in which you and others extended yourselves in many ways without expectation or hope of any compensation or return favors, consider that there is an accumulative effect to your efforts. If you develop a reputation for being trustworthy, cooperative, and someone who "gives good value," you are more likely to be chosen for opportunities that arise in the future. After all, wouldn't you prefer to work or associate with someone who is known for being fair, hardworking, and giving? Even if there is no immediate payoff to helping someone who probably can't reciprocate (you never know), your stock will go up as a valuable resource for others.

☐ Reciprocal Gains or Personal Satisfaction?

All this may sound rather cynical. Depending on how you define "doing good," this talk about helping others because you might someday enjoy some reciprocal favor is downright depressing. Certainly we are not often aware of our hidden motives when we extend ourselves to others.

Some helpers define doing good as more than merely extending yourself a little, or even performing a service for a fee. As illustrated in the following story of one helper, it represents a major commitment of energy and passion.

"I do something that someone finds helpful once in a while, but I'm no Peace Corps volunteer."

I stop her right there, think to myself that maybe she's right that we all have our disguised motives. Even the Peace Corps worker may have volunteered in the first place to bolster his or her resume and make him- or herself marketable, to run from an empty life, to hide from intimacy, or a whole assortment of escapist intentions that actually have little to do with anyone else.

I become lost in my own thoughts on the matter, then catch the thread again of what she is saying about how she helps people only on her own terms. I wonder what's so bad about that.

"I get really pissed when someone cuts me off or rides my butt while driving. I find myself ignoring most people I see who I would consider very needy. I think I'm not committed to doing good. I do good when it's convenient for me. When it comes right down to it, I'm actually no do-gooder. I don't like to see people suffer, but nor do I like to suffer. When I do good, it is because I can't *not* do whatever it is."

I see. So she is saying that she helps people to extinguish her own pain at watching others suffer. Certainly, that has a part in the choice to help. Altruism almost always involves reaching out to ourselves, as well as to others.

"Maybe an example would help," she offers. I nod enthusiastically.

"Someone in my art class was thinking of becoming a counselor and didn't know what it would take. No one in her family had ever gone to college so she didn't have a clue about the profession and its requirements. I told her what she wanted to know and this was extremely helpful for this woman. Yet it was no effort on my part. There was no personal sacrifice involved. I was bored so I gave her 15 minutes of my time. Big deal."

"That wasn't even doing good. While it wasn't 'doing bad' either, it certainly was doing good. The facts that I provided—those made a difference to her. But there was no effort in my heart. I think that making a difference and doing good involve some tugging at one's heart.

"I know this book is about how people devote their lives to helping others even when there isn't any personal gain—money or personal satisfaction."

It is at this point that I realize she has misunderstood what I am after. I thought she was going to say, "money and fame." But personal satisfaction? Gee, I thought that was what this was all about. I think to myself there is a big difference between reciprocal altruism, doing good in order to reap some reward, and doing good because you enjoy the feeling of helping others. I don't tell her any of this, but now I understand why she is being so hard on herself.

"Actually," she says with sadness in her voice, "I don't think I fall under this category. If I anticipate that I'll be personally dissatisfied by an act of helping, I won't do it. I've actually never realized how self-centered I am before reflecting on all of this. I've never realized how non-good-natured I am. True helping requires effort and sacrifice. I am having difficulty recalling times when I've done this."

Cost–Benefit Analysis

If you think kinship bonds and reciprocal altruism are cynical explanations for altruistic behavior, wait until you consider this next one, which looks at altruism as a special case of teamwork. Human beings are herd animals. Whether part of a tribe on the African plains or part of corporate culture, you can't make it alone. Predators tend to pick off stragglers rather than those who have found shelter in the middle of the pack. Unless you enjoy a network of support, contacts, and team members, you are not likely to be very successful.

Among lions, wolves, and other team predators, hunters work cooperatively to bring down prey, and they share in the spoils. This is not because they are generous, but because it is a more efficient expenditure of energy to accrue caloric rewards. Incredibly (I can hardly believe the serendipitous nature of the event), as I wrote this last sentence, the phone rang. A colleague was having difficulty completing an article he was working on; he felt stuck, discouraged, and wanted to gripe. I responded to his plea by asking if he wanted me to finish it for him, thinking this was his agenda. As it turns out, he was surprised by the offer, which was not at all what he had in mind. At first, I thought I was being generous and altruistic, but as the words left my mouth (perhaps because this subject is on my mind) I realized there was an implicit obligation in the offer that I would be expected to reciprocate by some day returning the favor of giving him a mostly completed article.

It may sound so petty, so harsh, so cold-blooded to help someone with the full expectation that the favor will be repaid. In actuality, we often don't think in that way. We help someone because it feels good to be useful. Yet, when you think of relationships in which you seem to be the one who is always initiating and giving, you likely feel cheated if not resentful.

Another variation of the cost–benefit equation takes place when people reason through the consequences of *not* helping others in need. "I couldn't live with myself," sounds at first like the reason offered by someone with a highly developed conscience, but it could also mean that he or she was really avoiding anticipatory guilt. Just as compelling are those who do good for others because they don't wish to appear selfish or foolish. This is especially the case if we are in the presence of family or friends when confronted with someone in distress.

The Many and the One

The previous explanations focus on how the individual benefits or suffers as a result of altruistic behavior. If you expand the view to include what is best for the community, then doing good must also be looked at in terms of its impact on others.

If we move away from humans for a minute and examine instead the cooperation among termites, bees, or ants, we see that the individual becomes meaningless. Such creatures are really a million connected minds, or segments of a central nervous system, that are all devoted to one goal such as repelling an enemy or finding food. "When they are all massed together," cellular biologist Lewis Thomas (1979) observed about ants, "all touching, exchanging bits of information held in their jaws like memoranda, they become a single animal.... One thing I'd like to know most of all: when those ants have made the Hill, and are all there ... and the whole mass begins to behave like a single huge creature, and *thinks*, what on earth is it that is thought?" (pp. 10–11).

We like to think of ourselves as so independent, individual, and autonomous, so much a product of our own free will, yet Thomas (1974) also mused in another essay whether we aren't all part of a much larger system. What if, he asks, our whole world is but a single cell in a larger organism? What if we are just bits of protoplasm with an inflated sense of self-importance?

Our purpose on this Earth may not at all be to further our egocentric, selfish goals but rather to serve the community and planet in the best way we can. If this sounds spiritual, it is meant to be. Yet there is no reason why evolution could not have played a part in programming us to be this way. Unless humans are devoted to helping one another, even when it involves tremendous sacrifices, we could not survive as a species even if our own offspring could make it to the next generation.

Human beings, and even primates, evolved the capacity for empathy because it is adaptive, helping us to quickly read others' moods in order to determine their intentions (Brothers, 1989). Empathy is what permits us to judge whether someone wishes to harm or help us and whether they like or fear us. One of the side effects of this ability to feel others' emotions is that we carry the burden of sensing their pain, a condition that is sometimes difficult to ignore unless we take some action. While this can involve closing our eyes and hearts to what we witness, the other option is to provide aid.

Whatever genetic programming we have that predisposes us to be helpful to others, this inclination is encouraged through cultural indoctrination to be generous, giving, and selfless. Smokey the Bear admonishes us not to light forest fires. We are told to "give to the United Way." Moral education teaches us to do the right thing. Certain religions require that congregants contribute a percentage of their income to charity; others teach that generosity is the ticket needed to get into heaven. Governments offer tax breaks to those who contribute money to noble causes. People who show great courage in sacrificing themselves for others are awarded medals for bravery and treated like heroes. The media regularly select and promote individuals who have engaged in some spectacular act of self-sacrifice. All of these cultural forces act to encourage individuals to put community interests above their personal needs. This is precisely the norm that has led millions of soldiers over the centuries to give their lives for their countries.

Justice and Empathy

People tend to behave in ways that are either extrinsically or intrinsically rewarding. If people choose to help someone, then there is likely to be some sort of payoff or such behavior would not continue. External rewards like recognition, approval, fame, and increased reputation, are somewhat obvious rewards. Far more complex are the internally based satisfactions that come from offering assistance: It feels good to help someone. Even if you receive not the slightest word of gratitude or the least recognition for your efforts, it still seems like a good thing to do.

In some cases, heroic individuals have not only acted without concern for rewards but have actually hidden from the limelight. For example, Lenny Skutnik was driving home from work one stormy, winter night in Washington, D.C. An Air Florida plane crashed right before his eyes, smack into the Potomac River, where survivors began drowning and freezing to death. While spectators and even camera crews looked on in horror, Skutnik dived into the icy river to rescue floundering passengers. Afterwards, he was embarrassed by any attention he received, refused to sell his story, and did his best to slide back into obscurity.

While Skutnik survived his heroic acts, another man, Arland Williams, went even one step further. On that same horrific night, he was one of the unfortunate passengers who ended up floundering for his life hanging on to the tail section of the plane floating in the river. When a helicopter arrived to rescue him and four other freezing victims, he willingly allowed the others to be pulled up first, knowing that he would most likely die as a result.

This behavior, however laudable, is also completely incomprehensible, noted Hunt (1990) in his book on the mysteries of altruism. This is more than a little strange. Why on earth would someone willingly die for a bunch of strangers? Did he have a death wish? Was he insane? After all, you'd have to be a little nuts to risk your life in such a way, wouldn't you?

Williams isn't around to interview, to find out why he did what he did, but there are plenty of other heroes alive who can answer for him. What is often said by such individuals when queried as to their motives is that it just seemed like the right thing to do. There was an absence of thought, of course, otherwise a voice inside the head would scream very loudly: "Are you crazy? Save yourself, and me too!"

In a review of the literature related to altruism, Piliavin and Charng (1990) debunk the myth that humans in general, and children in particular, are inherently self-centered and egocentric, citing evidence of sharing at the earliest age. They conclude that altruism, and our capacity to feel empathy and concern for others, is indeed part of human nature.

There is some evidence that humans are genetically disposed to feel empathic arousal in response to others' distress (Hoffman, 1990; Zahn-Waxler, Radke-Yarrow, Wagner, & Chapman, 1992). This means that discomfort can be reduced by either blocking out the scene or offering assistance.

Brehony (1999) confirmed this with her own research, documenting case after case in which ordinary individuals risked their safety and lives in order to help complete strangers. Furthermore, acts of grace are so common they are taken for granted. "Among the people I interviewed and studied," she writes, "there is a clear understanding that goodness resides in every human being, no matter how difficult it may be to see" (Brehony, 1999, p. 43).

In talking about the role of empathy, a European teacher describes what it means in her work.

"Here I come to think of a quotation by Soren Kierkegaard, that I know both in Danish and Icelandic, but not in English. It is on the art of helping and explains very well the essence of empathy. It says something like, 'When, in truth, you want to guide or lead a person to a specific point, you first of all have to find out where he or she is and start the journey there.' To me, this is the secret of helping. In order to help someone else, I must understand more than he or she does, but first and foremost I must understand what he or she understands. If I don't do this, then my greater understanding doesn't help at all."

Human beings are born with the capacity to feel *for* others, called sympathy, and *with* others, known as empathy. The difference between these two is a matter of emotion matching or degree of personal investment (Sober & Wilson, 1998). *Empathy* involves taking another's perspective, identifying emotionally with his or her plight, feeling the pain, whereas *sympathy* is a more objective, detached state. In both cases, you feel a degree of motivation to reach out and help someone.

Altruism is motivated, in part, by empathic arousal—the vicarious emotional response to others' pain or helplessness (Hoffman, 1981). When someone is distressed, you feel badly for them (sympathy), sometimes to the point where you imagine what it's like to *be* in their position. Under such circumstances, one way to reduce your own discomfort is to come to the aid of the other.

If we could slow down this process as it is actually occurring inside someone's head, and if unconscious thoughts were brought more fully into awareness, we might hear an internal dialogue such as the following when confronted with an individual in obvious distress.

What's going on here? Gee, he seems upset about something.... I'm gonna be late. Gotta get going....

I wonder if someone else can do something about this? This guy really seems to be having a hard time. I sure know what that's like. I remember ...

He's probably okay. He just needs some time to be alone. Besides, there's probably nothing I can do anyway....

My heart aches for this guy. He looks so alone. He sees all these people passing him by, nobody who cares enough to stop. Maybe I could....

No, I really gotta run....

You can easily see the dilemma between self-interest and offering help that comes with a cost. While such an internal debate would rarely be this explicit, the example illustrates the alternating motives between taking care of one's own needs and those of someone else. It is empathic resonance that captures attention and maintains it to the point that altruistic behavior will more likely take place. Even if this person walks away from the scene, deciding to keep the appointment, there will likely be a price to pay in the form of residual guilt and emotional arousal.

It is probable that if you are considering a life devoted to service, empathy plays a big part in your decision. You may have developed this capacity via your own painful life experiences, through growing up in a household that was rich in this dimension, or perhaps as an innate gift that allows you to sense what others are feeling. You are probably deeply affected (whether you show it or not) when in the presence of someone else's distress.

Regardless of your current empathic ability, much of learning to be an effective helper involves heightening this sensitivity so that you may be better able to crawl inside someone else's skin and imagine what he or she must be going through. This is what permits you to form accurate readings about what another person is feeling, and then to reflect back what you sense is going on. Of course, one of the skills of professional helpers, distinguished from amateurs, is their ability to set clear boundaries between themselves and others so they don't overpersonalize to the point where they experience deleterious effects.

One experienced therapist describes this struggle:

"When I first started out in the field I could feel everything. Too much. I couldn't turn it [the client's suffering] off. I thought so much about the people I was helping that I couldn't sleep at night. I worried constantly. I thought this meant that I was good at my job, that I cared so much.

"My supervisor confronted me on this stuff by telling me that I wasn't helping my clients worrying about them so I must have been doing it to help myself in some way. I thought he was being a real jerk at the time, but the more I thought about it, the more I realized that carrying my clients' pain did two things. One, it made me feel needed and important. And two, as long as I thought about their stuff, I didn't have to think about my own."

A bit later we will look in greater detail at other sacrifices that are made to be empathic and helpful. For now, it's important to understand that empathy can be your greatest gift—or burden—depending on how skilled you become at separating other people's issues from your own. This takes a lot of practice and the guidance of a supportive, honest supervisor.

Moral Imperatives

If sympathy and empathy act as motivators to help, then so do moral principles that have been internalized. Education in the form of parental, school, religious, spiritual, and community values teaches us about what it means to be a good citizen. "Do unto others as you would have them do unto you." "Be a good neighbor." "Thou shalt not steal." Our minds and hearts are filled with such imperatives that guide our choices and often lead us to reach out to others.

In one study of altruists including philanthropists and heroes and heroines, Monroe (1996) asked people why they gave away their fortunes or risked their lives for the sake of others. The reasons given parallel the range of moral developmental stages from the most primitive level of guilt avoidance to principled conscience. While some of the respondents said things like, "I couldn't have lived with myself otherwise," "What would people say?," or "I had no choice," others acted generously to see the joy on people's faces. More often than not, the concepts of empathy and justice were mentioned: "I felt bad for the person. It was the right thing to do."

Love

There are certain personality characteristics associated with those who are altruistic (Jeffries, 1998; S. P. Oliner & Oliner, 1988; Rushton, 1981). Such individuals consistently demonstrate compassion, kindness, caring, self-sacrifice, and love in their efforts to be helpful to others. They think nothing about helping little old ladies (and men) across the street. They contribute large sums, and large blocks of time, to charitable causes. They look for opportunities to reach out to others. They devote their lives to doing good. They are often filled with love for others, not only those they count among friends and family, but even those they have never met. Furthermore, they neither expect nor ask for anything in return.

One such individual, a nun working in the slums of Calcutta, tried to ease the pain and discomfort of lepers who had nowhere else to go. "The scene was straight out of Dante's *Inferno*," writes Lapierre (1985, p. 386) in his chronicle of attempting to do good in the *City of Joy*. "Hardly had a leper placed his stump on the table than a swarm of maggots would come crawling out of it ... Sister Gabrielle acted as anesthetist. She had nothing to relieve the pain of certain amputations—no morphine—no curare or bhang. She had only her love." While the doctor would saw off putrefied limbs, Sister Gabrielle would hold the lepers in her arms, singing them lullabies.

There would seem to be certain people who hold a strong sense of equity and generosity, almost as a part of their personalities. In reviewing the research to date on so-called altruistic personalities, especially among children who show early signs of doing good for others, Hunt (1990) found that the following characteristics were most often in evidence:

1. Happy, well-adjusted, popular kids were more likely to be helpful to others than those who are sad, isolated, or in bad moods.
2. Young children who are emotionally expressive and sensitive are more likely to respond to others in trouble.
3. High self-esteem was associated with helpful acts, since people are more inclined to extend themselves to others who they perceive as worse off than they are.

While the evidence is not overwhelming, there seems to be indications that some people have altruistic personalities, or natural inclinations to do good for others. They appear to be infused with love for others, even those they have never met.

Rarely does anyone mention love in the professional literature. It is too "soft" and unscientific, and nobody is quite sure what it is exactly. Bemak and Epp (1996) believe that love is one of the major curative factors that operate in helping efforts. Breggin (1997) calls it the central guiding impulse of human life, a basic need to give to others. He defines it as a kind of "joyful awareness" that takes place between people who share intimate experiences. That is not unlike what Moore (1994) describes as a "soulful relationship," one in which there is a profound connection, a deep communion that seems to transcend intentional efforts to a state of divine grace.

Surely you can recall such an encounter with someone you were helping. There must have been an instance in your life when you were at the right place at the right time to be of service to someone in need. The relationship that evolved, the help you provided, cemented you together in a way that nothing else could. Even if you never saw this person again, your love and compassion remain timeless.

A marketing executive walks around the planet looking for opportunities to be helpful to others. These gestures become easier and easier for her to initiate once she realizes that the satisfaction she gets is no longer dependent on how, or if, the needy person responds.

"I tend to look forward to those spontaneous moments that come without forethought when I come to someone's defense—I literally spent two full days in court testifying for a complete stranger who was kicked by a tow truck driver in front of a police officer in front of my home. I also remember an old woman crossing a busy street near where I live and tripping with a bag of groceries—spilling its contents all over the pavement. Cars honked at me because I'd blocked some traffic as I stopped to help her up, carry her groceries to the curb where I asked her to wait while I pulled my car over to the side. I was appalled by the number of expletives yelled at me during those short minutes. I managed to escort the woman to her apartment, wash up her cuts, put away the groceries, and we enjoyed an hour of tea and cookies. I think I missed a meeting that day, but I enjoy remembering what I didn't miss more."

Within a helping encounter such as this, love takes a different form than what we ordinarily associate with romantic, parental, or even friendship attachment. It is a nondemanding type of caring in which the helper does not meet his or her own needs. It is what Ram Das and Gorman (1985) refer to as *compassionate caring*, a joining together of spirits. This is one of the features of a helping relationship that makes it so special and healing. At no time does the person being helped have to wonder about being exploited, manipulated, or taken advantage of.

I suppose that is why we give love a different name in helping, to distinguish it from the type of passion and arousal that take place in romantic and family relationships. Yet terms like compassion and empathy don't quite capture the essence of what it means to reach out of yourself and offer help to another. It takes the words of practitioners who do this type of work to flesh out the deeper meaning—not only of love, but caring, altruism, compassion, empathy, justice, and commitment.

Voices of Those Who Help

When you put these concepts together, you have both biological and cultural influences that encourage people to do good for others. Some of the altruistic motives meet the criteria mentioned by the helper in the previous chapter: They involve a *major* investment of energy and commitment, as well as involvement of the heart. While there may be some personal satisfaction or benefit that results from the effort, such motives are not conscious or very prominent.

In this chapter, we listen to the voices of people who sing the glory of doing good for the most noble purposes. In the next chapter, we will examine, as well, the parts of us that do good for others because of some personal gain. This distinction is arbitrary. It is more often the case that we do good for both altruistic *and* selfish reasons, even if we are not aware of these motives.

If altruistic forces did not exert such power, our whole society would be in danger of falling apart. So while evolutionary theory offers some interesting speculation about why we are inclined to extend ourselves to others without hope of an immediate payoff, either for ourselves or our immediate kin, it does not cover the whole territory.

If you talk to enough people who devote themselves to service, whether as professionals (counselors, therapists, clergy, etc.) volunteers, philanthropists, or just compassionate, concerned citizens, you will hear a variety of reasons for their commitment. Each of these motives is supported by the voices of experienced helpers.

☐ Being Part of Something Bigger Than Yourself

It can be a very lonely, isolated world, one in which we feel locked in what Howard (1975) described as a "flesh-colored cage." Each of us is a separate being, born alone, and will die alone. During the interval between those two points we search for something greater than ourselves, some way to give our lives personal meaning. The act of helping often provides that sense of being part of something so much bigger than your own little world. In part, this can act as a distraction from your own troubles, but far more than that, helping provides a grander perspective on life.

A teacher and specialist in group leadership likes the idea that he can leave himself, his problems and preoccupations, when he fully enters into a helping activity. He becomes less self-involved and more completely alive:

"This may seem like a strange story about serving others, because athletics have a negative connotation, but for me it all started with playing baseball as a kid.

"Here is what it was like. I am standing on the pitcher's mound on a warm summer evening totally oblivious to all around me except the threads on the ball and how best to place fingers on them. I fix all of my attention on the next batter's practice swing and my memory of his hitting weaknesses and strengths. I study the catcher's glove and the signs he is giving me. Then I begin my windup.

"The ball springs out of my hand toward the plate, and for a moment, time stands still as I await my fate. Hours pass in moments, and the game ends. I have just lived 2 hours of total commitment, focused concentration, and full purpose. Who was served in the process? It didn't matter to me then and doesn't now when I counsel, teach, or help someone.

"In retrospect, I suppose these games brought the adults and children in our small town together with a greater sense of community. Today, the classroom is my pitcher's mound and I'd like to think I'm still doing my part to bring people together."

It is the theme of doing your part, contributing something meaningful, that you will hear again and again in the narratives that follow. The motives for helping are far more complex than that, however. In some cases, people reach out to others because it seems like the most natural thing in the world to do at the time.

☐ It Comes Naturally

Some people who work in many fields spend a portion of their lives volunteering their time in service to others. They feel an obligation, of sorts, to do it because they can and because they feel it is their responsibility to give something back. A journalist and philanthropist describes how she has made helping a part of her lifestyle:

"First, I don't really consider anything I have ever done to help others as work. I don't do this because I have to, but because I want to. Secondly, I don't really have any formal training helping others—it's more instinctual for me. It just seems to be the right thing to do, and it's something I thoroughly enjoy. I don't give the process a whole lot of thought in all honesty. It's just part of living life for me. It's what I do."

Indeed, it is what she does, what we all do because it seems like what we were meant to do. There is a strong need that most of us feel to give something back, to extend ourselves to others. Rationally and consciously, our actions don't always make sense. In fact, the woman just described doesn't even like thinking about why she helps others—the analysis seems to diminish the pleasure she feels.

☐ To Touch Another

Continuing the theme of reaching outside of ourselves to connect with others, there is an essential intimacy that takes place in a helping encounter. It is quite unlike any other relationship, but one that is both exhilarating and frightening.

An ex-teacher, ex-therapist, ex-educator, now retired, has devoted her whole life to helping others because it is simply part of who she is. Even now, she still volunteers a significant part of her time mentoring and supervising beginning helpers, refusing to accept payment for her services. She reasons she has been paid enough in her life, has no need for any more money, and so revels in the freedom to do good whenever and wherever the spirit moves her.

"My desire to help comes from a place of caring, sensitivity, thoughtfulness, almost a necessity to give love to others. It feels part of who I am."

When asked to supply an example that best represents what it means for her to do good, she feels flooded with images that come to mind:

"There have been so many in my life, but there is one person who stands out, mostly because everyone else gave up on her. This was a fairly disturbed young woman, very dysfunctional, perhaps even qualified as a full-fledged borderline disorder.

"I went so far beyond what I was supposed to do for her. She had been hospitalized after I had referred her to a psychiatrist, so she was no longer my responsibility. Technically, she wasn't my patient any more. Some time after she was released, maybe a year or two after I had last seen her, she called me one day and asked if she could come by and give me something. At first, I was leery. I didn't want to set a precedent, knowing that she could start playing with other boundaries and intrude in my life. But I cared about this woman deeply, so I agreed to meet with her for a few minutes.

"All she wanted from me was a hug. That's it! We said a few words to one another. She gave me a stuffed animal that she wanted me to keep for her. We hugged. Then she walked out the door. Didn't look back. That was, oh, maybe 6 years ago."

This retired helper is just in awe of the power that comes from a simple, caring hug. In one sense, it seems like she has really done so little even though the act means so much.

"She comes by my house about two or three times a year," the educator continues with a fond smile of satisfaction on her face. "Makes an appointment. We don't say hardly anything to one another. I just ask her how she's doing. She replies that she is doing extremely well, very successful in her work. Then we hug and she leaves. She says these hugs sustain her, that they have been the foundation upon which she has made such fantastic progress."

She shakes her head as she retells the story, not at all sure that anyone could truly appreciate the seemingly magical transformation that has taken place.

"I don't delude myself in the force of a simple hug. Neither do I minimize its power. But I *know* I've made a difference with her."

She says this was such conviction, such certainty. There is none of the doubt expressed by the woman earlier who wonders if she can ever know she helped anyone. By contrast, there are few things about which this retired helper can feel more sure than the certainty that she has been useful.

"It's always been this way," she says, "ever since I was a kid. It's always been important to me to impact others in a helpful, positive way. That's the reward for me. It fills me with ... I don't know if it's pride or pleasure or ... I can't quite describe it. But I'm emotionally filled with love at being able to touch another."

I know a male psychologist who is the exact opposite of this retired educator, at least in terms of basic philosophy and helping approach. Whereas she is a self-avowed radical humanist, he is a staunch behaviorist and empiricist, a specialist in neuropsychological assessment and technology. It is therefore affirming to hear him describe almost the same kind of experience he enjoys as a result of his work:

"A few months ago I received a note from a person whose name I did not recognize. Caution suggests not opening such correspondence, but my curiosity won out. The message was from a client whom I had seen briefly, more than 20 years ago, in another state. This contact is at the heart of what it means to me to be a helper of others even though I did not even remember having worked with her!

"The case itself was not particularly noteworthy. From her message, however, it was evident that in just a few hours of shared experience, a relationship was formed, a connection strong enough to warrant her going to significant effort to find me. There perhaps can be no greater satisfaction than knowing that you have touched someone's life, helped them make it through a difficult time, and inspired confidence to the extent that the individual makes extraordinary effort to seek your assistance again in a time of personal distress."

☐ The Relationships

In the previous stories, the helpers allude to the power of the relationships they developed with others, connections that were so strong they seemed to be at the heart of whatever help they offered. This theme is also echoed in the tale of an Australian teacher who works with troubled boys as a volunteer:

"I suppose the tangible rewards are nonexistent [from this work] but the relationships are truly rewarding whether I help them [the children] become more successful at school or not. These boys never leave you in doubt about how they are feeling and what they think. I really respect this in them even though it is hard to accept all that they do and say. Being able to deal with human beings that do not want to hide their feelings is a great joy for me. You know where you stand and this is so refreshing. The fact that I can relate to these boys when others cannot makes me happy as I know that it is not impossible to help even if the situation is difficult."

This teacher is describing a special kind of relationship he has been able to develop with the kids he helps. It has all the familiar elements that you learn about (and will be described in detail later) in standard texts. There is a degree of mutual respect, trust, acceptance, and consistency that is present, qualities that take both time and lots of commitment to nurture. It is obvious that this hasn't been easy for him to do, especially since others have long given up on these kids. But it is these relationships that he values most of all.

☐ Diminishing Own Problems

Our field attracts its share of wounded healers, people who have experienced great suffering or who prefer to get their counseling vicariously rather than directly. I suppose it is fair to say that we all have our problems and issues that we have not fully resolved. More than a few helpers I've interviewed admitted, reluctantly at first, that they secretly enjoy working with people who are worse off than they are: It makes you feel better about your own life.

One therapist from New Zealand talks about how good, capable, and worthwhile he feels when he is helping others.

"It gives my life significant meaning. If there is another human being brightened because of my presence it was all worth the scariness of somebody considering ending his or her life."

Similar to an earlier disclosure, this therapist likes the way helping gets him outside of himself and his own narrow world.

"I can forget my own struggles for a while as I immerse myself in another's life. I can appreciate just how good my life is, difficult as the challenges might be."

Indeed, one of the benefits we enjoy from this type of work is that we are permitted an intimate look into the most private worlds of others. We hear their secrets, their most confidential stories, their tales of heartbreak, misery, and frustration. Inside, we can't help but make comparisons to what we are living through, and such introspection is quite revealing. There you are feeling sorry for yourself because you can't buy the car you really want and you meet someone who is fighting to find enough food to eat. Or you are worried about an upcoming assignment or meeting, and you hear the story of someone who is struggling with cancer. Your own troubles often seem pitifully trite in comparison to the needy people you encounter. This most certainly introduces an alternative perspective on things.

☐ Getting a Different Perspective

We are often changed as much as our clients during the helping process. We hear their stories and we are profoundly affected by them. When we talk to them, we are also talking to ourselves. It is a relationship that constantly moves in both directions.

"What is love?" asks a psychologist and diagnostician who specializes in assessment interviews. "Through the lens of behavioral science, it is a self-constructed explanation for a feeling state when there is no biological explanation for the feeling, manipulated through expectations of increased probability of positive future consequences."

Speaking the language of his behaviorist roots, I wasn't sure what he was trying to say in the content of that statement. Was he saying that he felt love for his clients? Certainly not, I thought, considering the rather objective style he employed in his work and interactions. Then he clarified further that he was really talking about the multiple perceptual shifts that are possible when a helper adopts an empathic stance. He likens this to a metaphor of lenses:

"But through a different lens, it is an inexplicable experiential bonding which helps bring meaning to life. Which lens is best? A primary benefit which my work affords is that I have continuing opportunity to view the world through each of these vantage points. I am not forced to choose between the two perspectives. Instead, as a psychotherapist and diagnostician, I have continuing opportunities to recognize, use, and even contribute to the science of human behavior while at the same time acknowledging that the human experience exceeds the inherent limitations of a single lens."

This type of work we do constantly challenges us to integrate others' points of view with our own perspectives. We are working philosophers, but the sort who are continuously evolving our ideas in light of new experiences, new data, and conflicting perspectives. While it is sometimes confusing and disorienting to face things that directly or indirectly conflict with our most cherished beliefs, a growing practitioner is one who remains open and flexible.

☐ Making Contact

The experience of helping others sometimes transports us to another dimension, one in which we feel the most perfect contact with the larger world. It is at such times that we feel most connected to those around us.

An international consultant works to build linkages for professional exchanges between North and South America. During one visit to Columbia, he was invited to visit the premier psychiatric hospital to discuss opportunities where he might be most helpful.

"I was driven there in a chauffeured car, accompanied by government high officials who wanted to impress me," the consultant says with a mixture of awe and discomfort. "The hospital was a former convent, with a large castle-like structure made out of old stone. The views all around were magnificent. Mountains and clear sky. It seemed like such a serene place."

"We went into the locked gates directly to the fourth floor," he continues, lost in memories of an experience that was obviously as disturbing as it was exhilarating. It was midday so an exquisite lunch was prepared. We sat in an opulent conference room, socializing and talking about business."

"I glanced out the window and caught my first view of the patients down below. Thousands of them huddled in the courtyard, in rags, naked, some with shoes, most without anything on their feet.

"When the hospital administrators caught me looking at the patients, they quickly ushered me away, not wanting me to be disturbed by this chaos. I thought about how this has been the same story throughout most of my life, just laid out here before me in a perfect metaphor. Down below were these human beings who were the focus of our discussions, while we sat at the top, the fourth floor, as if on a different planet. We were deciding their lives, their future, without knowing what is in their hearts and souls.

"I insisted that I wanted to meet the residents, but was quickly told that was impossible. 'But doctor,' they told me, 'they don't speak English.... It is not so clean.... You really don't want to go down there.' Finally, as a last resort when they saw I was not to be dissuaded, they said 'It is not safe.'

"Visiting dignitaries have a way of getting what they want so eventually I prevailed. The whole entourage accompanied me into the mass of humanity, hundreds of institutionalized psychiatric patients.

"I found no less than what I have encountered throughout the world, the same that I always find in these moments. Hungry eyes. Grabbing hands looking to touch, and be touched. Smiles coming up from tired souls, looking for hope. Around me, my colleagues were uncomfortable, even scared, worried about being hurt or soiled. Yet I felt like I was floating. I was really seeing these people and I felt seen by them as well. This, to me, is the essence of service."

Indeed, the deep, direct, intimate contact with others is one of the benefits, as well as a burden, of helping others. In this process of joining people in their struggles, we see them and are seen, even when we prefer to hide.

☐ Giving Something Back

So many helpers talk about the struggles and pain that they too have suffered in their lives. Someone reached out to them at a time of need, providing the care and mentoring that made it possible for them to survive, even flourish. This could have been a teacher, a coach, a counselor or therapist, even a stranger who showed them the way out of their misery.

I know this has been the case in my own life. I suffered terrible doubts and shyness as a child. I had little confidence that I could do anything very well; I was neither an athlete, nor did I appear very bright. In fact, framed on the wall of my office is my nursery school diploma and first report card. I received satisfactory grades in all the basic subjects—from table work to nap time—but under intelligence, it says "average" with a question mark. I was a "special ed" kid before they had special classes. I was shy, insecure, and mediocre in everything I did. Even my parents gave up on me.

A teacher decided I showed promise and decided to nurture me along the way. Later, my school counselor took an interest and got me into a college (on probation because of my terrible grades). A professor mentored me. Then, during a bout with depression over a lost love, a therapist helped me get through my early adulthood. Through all these times, it took the patience and support of several devoted helpers to get me on solid footing.

Finally, I found my own way. And to this day I am so grateful for the assistance I got along the way that it seemed only fair that I devote my life to pay back my mentors by helping other lost souls who are like me.

Another story is told by a foster parent who takes children who have yet to be adopted. She talked about where the spirit of helping first originated.

"When I was 10, my mother died unexpectedly, leaving me with three older brothers and a father with whom I did not have a close relationship. As one might imagine, all of the sadness and fear related to my mother's death was particularly salient during holidays and birthdays. On my 11th birthday, 6 months after my mother's death, a neighbor appeared with a Red Velvet Cake to share.

"Perhaps because of the sadness in her own life, this neighbor seemed to understand my pain and sadness, and especially how difficult birthdays would be for me. She never spoke to me directly about her wisdom, yet her offering of cake communicated the hope and caring I needed in my life at the time. Her gift showed me that life goes on despite how difficult it can be at times, and that there are people in the world who would take care of me during the most difficult and scary times. The Red Velvet Cake became a tradition for me (and my brother)—after that first cake our neighbor never missed a child's birthday!

"I don't know if she ever appreciated the profound impact of her gesture toward me at such a difficult time in my life. I am quite sure that her gift to me laid the foundation for my commitment to giving to others—a commitment that has had a profound impact on my life as an adult. And in honor of this neighbor, each of my children has a Red Velvet Cake for their birthday each year. Sometimes they ask for me to color it purple, or yellow, or green, but regardless of its color, her spirit is always present.

"My work with others is like Red Velvet Cake—however humble, it is made with care and aimed at making a small difference in the life of others. I have no illusions that my helping others provides the hope and inspiration that my neighbor's gesture gave to me during my childhood, but I do know that my life is filled with joy and a sense of meaning with each effort that I make to reach out to others.

"Eleven years ago and just days after our foster-parent training program, a social worker asked my husband and I to take in our first foster children: two brothers, ages 9 and 13. Her hope was that the two boys would learn how to become a part of a family. A modest aspiration, it may seem, but she had her doubts. They had been in a number of foster homes and most recently disrupted from an adoption placement. The fear was that their discouragement would prevent them from bonding with adults and prohibit eventual adoption.

"Raising those boys for the 9 months before they were adopted was an unanticipated gift! As we helped them adapt to their circumstances, learn about the birds and the bees, and make some very difficult decisions, as we traveled with them across the country and hung out with them in the day-to-day homework checking and woke up before work and school each day to help the oldest with his paper route, they gave us the gift of joy that only parents can feel when they work and play with their children. We knew that they were able to become a part of a family when we became aware of how difficult it was to let go of them so that they could move on. In recent conversations with their adoptive parents (11 years later) came the confirmation that we learned not to expect from our humble efforts to make a difference in the lives of others: They both successfully graduated from high school and are moving nicely along in their chosen career paths!"

It is as though the gift of doing good keeps on giving, from one generation to the next. Sometimes, it's like a game of "pass it on" in which someone does something nice for you so you pass on this goodness to others. But it's hardly a game; it's the single most real act a human can do for another.

☐ Community of Caring

Some people do good for others because that's the way they were raised. They grew up in a family or community in which it was expected that you take care of everyone, just as they will take care of you. This moral code becomes part of your very fiber as described by one counselor who grew up in a rural area:

"I grew up on a cattle ranch in northeast Colorado. It was an isolated, sparsely populated area where helping one another was the normal and necessary way of being. When our corn was ready to harvest, another rancher who didn't raise corn helped drive trucks. When we had blizzards, neighbors actively checked on one another and responded to various needs of the community members. Ranches were huge and miles apart; thus this level of neighbor caring for neighbors was by no means convenient.

"I remember a caravan of 4-wheel-drive trucks going to town 45 miles away in dangerous weather to get medicine and supplies for community members. After the blizzard my dad delivered mail to stranded, elderly neighbors for 6 weeks. In the context of autonomous, independent, robust ranch families, there was a deep and sincere sense of community that still prevails today.

"Several years ago, I learned about a private but lovely tradition that grew from that community. The tradition started many years ago when a retiring rancher loaned a significant amount of money to a young couple who were buying their first cattle ranch. The older man would not accept interest. Rather, he said, 'When you get on your feet, you can do the same for someone else in need.' I found out about this tradition after my home burned. I received $2,000 in the mail with the story of the tradition. That experience changed my life in many ways."

Not only has this ritual of people taking care of one another changed her life, but the ripple effects have multiplied when you consider the number of people she has helped since then and how many others still continue the tradition of passing the help along to others in need. That is the amazing thing about doing good—how contagious it can become!

☐ A Legacy

In a sense, helpers are immortal. As long as you continue to live in the grateful memories of those you have assisted, your spirit continues. Teachers know this and revel in the satisfaction when students return years later to thank them for what they learned. The behavioral psychologist who spoke earlier also mentioned the kick he got out of hearing years later from a client he didn't even remember who was so positively impacted by their work together.

It is a gift we receive when we know we have made a difference in someone's life. Even more satisfying are those times when the other person acknowledges our help and thanks us profusely. Still more astounding is when this person can even point to what we did that mattered most.

A supervisor and educator of counselors talks about how good it feels when she receives such praise from those she mentors:

"I don't worry about cancer, heart disease, potential death by accidents, or other personal disasters, and little at all about financial matters. Sure I take care of myself and I'm comfortably middle class, though savings and investments are zilch. But I see many others who take even better care and they are often overwhelmed with anxieties over money, health, and avoidance of any number of risks to jeopardize their financial or physical life status. What is different about me from my perspective?

"One of the things I see as different is that much of my life has been helping others and I have seen the work pay off for them. I'm at peace with myself because of it. If I knew that I would die tomorrow, I would feel good about my life, what I have given, and what goes on because of it. I feel like I could leave the world with the knowledge that I have helped, that people carry my ideas and benefits with them, that I have done good, and that I have had to ask for little from others. I don't owe any debts to people and have given more than I have taken. It is among the most satisfying and comforting thoughts I can have.

"The other piece of how helping others feels very good to me is the recognition that although the major paybacks for this work don't often come when you do the help, they do seem to come later, and sometimes much later. It is the phone call, or letter, or request to speak, or someone stopping by after a month, a year, or 10 years to say how much I helped, even though they hadn't expressed or maybe even recognized it at the time. These gifts of fresh life rarely come at the time of helping or at appointed holidays. They come later, at random times and in unexpected ways. It takes patience to not ask for the gifts and not be disappointed when they don't come at times when I could really use them. But when they do come without request they make it all worthwhile."

Yes, it is so lovely when our help is acknowledged, and even better when we receive gratitude. I disagree with this counselor supervisor, at least based on my experience, that such feedback gifts are so common. I have found that if you expect such gratitude, if you need it in order to feel fulfilled, you are going to be frequently disappointed. Sure, it is wonderful when someone thanks us for our efforts, especially with the degree of enthusiasm that we would prefer, but unfortunately, all too often our work goes unrecognized and unappreciated. Those you do help may not be willing to acknowledge the assistance. When they do thank you, it might surprise you that it is for something that you don't even remember doing. That is why it is so important to accrue internal satisfaction from your work—the thanks you get from others will never be nearly enough.

Another well-advised strategy is to take what gratitude you can get from the subtle, nonverbal acknowledgments you will see in people's faces and hear in their voices.

"I do this for the smiles," admits a grantwriter who works with street children in impoverished areas. "It's always their smiles that hook me. These are kids who have been given an emotional death sentence. All life is beaten and starved out of them. They have no hope.

"There are times when I can see them coming alive again. They are reawakening. . . . No, they are reborn into an existence that couldn't even be imagined. To watch and participate in this transformation is the most precious gift."

☐ To Save a Life

There is a bit of a rescuer in all of us. We have this fantasy that because we were at the right place at the right time we can somehow be instrumental in saving someone's life just at the moment when this person had given up all hope. Even if you never talk someone off the ledge of a tall building or jump into a deep lake to save a drowning victim, metaphorically that is what we hope to do when we see someone suffering. They are indeed drowning in their misery or about to take a destructive leap without a safety net, and we are their only potential rescuer. Damn if it doesn't feel good to save a life!

A nurse who volunteers her time for various charitable organizations talks about the commitment to caring that goes beyond her professional roles. She remembers one time she was working for Meals on Wheels, delivering food to homebound senior citizens.

"When you deliver a route enough times, you get to know your clients and their little idiosyncrasies. I had this one elderly client who had a great deal of trouble walking. So, every Friday my driver and I would pull up into her driveway, her drapes would be open and her door could be shut or open, but always unlocked. One day, my driver pulled up to her house and immediately I noticed that her morning paper was still hanging from the doorknob on the front door. I also noticed that her drapes were shut. I told the driver that this didn't look right. I got out and tried the door but it was locked. I looked in all the windows I could reach. I couldn't see her anywhere. After about 20 minutes, and several calls to the office, I was able to locate a neighbor who had a key to the house. When I walked inside I found the woman lying on the floor in the hallway. She had fallen off the edge of her bed and couldn't get up, so she scooted into the hallway. That had been about 6 hours earlier!

"I called an ambulance to come and get her. Before they wheeled her away, she said to me in a barely audible voice, 'Did you hear me screaming?' I said, 'Honey, I couldn't hear a thing. I just knew you were in there and I wasn't leaving until I found you.'"

Of course, we aren't really as powerful as we think we are. Maybe in this case, the nurse really did save a life. With most of us, however, we aren't really "saving" anybody as much as we are helping them to save themselves. After all, they are the ones doing most of the work.

☐ Next to Godliness

There is often a spiritual mission associated with doing good, as if it is God's work. This is not only cited by members of the clergy, or conventionally religious people, but by others who feel infused by a Higher Power in their helping efforts.

"It's very difficult to trace from where I got this strong sense of helping," says a counselor and educator. "I was raised by an aunt who spent her life helping others. There was a belief in our African-American community that helping was next to Godliness."

We are back to the theme raised earlier by the educator who grew up in the ranch country of Colorado. When you are brought up to do good, it just seems the most natural thing to do. In this case, however, instead of feeling primary commitment to the community, it is directed instead to devotion to God.

This counselor reminisces: "My aunt Johnnie would make me recite statements like "No matter how much you give, you can't be God giving." If people came to our house while we were eating, we had to share—even if there was barely enough for us. While growing up, my family and I visited the sick, fed the hungry, took in strays, shared our time, energy, and money with those who needed it most.

"When I was about 10 or 11, my aunt—who was really my mother—told me to go help an elderly lady clean her house. I spent the entire day washing dishes, dusting, mopping, sweeping, and so on. At the end of the day, the old lady offered me some money—about 50 cents—and I had to say 'No thank you.' If I had taken the money, my Aunt would have disapproved and made me return it. She believed that my reward was in the giving."

One can be raised to do "God's work" of helping, such as the type of service missions expected of those who are members of particular religious faiths, or choose this path as an adult. I talked with one young couple who were on their way to staff a mission in a small village in Tanzania. They had already lived and worked there for a number of years, ministering to the needs of a population with an HIV infection rate of over 50%. Yet, they didn't feel like they were making any great sacrifice. "It's just what God wants us to do," they said with total conviction.

Once religious beliefs are brought into the picture, the question of motive becomes a lot more complex. There are those who go on missions, give away fortunes to charity, or work on behalf of their churches or temples not so much because they are all that interested in helping people, but because they see it as a ticket to heaven. They believe God is watching, keeping score, waiting to decide whether they have accrued enough altruistic points to qualify for eternal salvation. In a sense, their work is no different from a helper who is working primarily for a salary.

Compare the difference, for instance, between two 20-year-old missionaries in Mexico City. One of them speaks with genuine fervor that this is the highlight of his young life, that he really feels that what he is doing is the most important thing he will ever do. His companion shares this conviction, at least outwardly; privately, however, he confides that the real reason he is doing the mission is because it is expected in his family. "Besides," he says with mischievous twinkle, "it's the only way to get a good wife when I come back."

Of course, in all of us, even those who appear the most pure and sanctimonious in their motives, there are both intrinsic and extrinsic rewards. It is important to be honest with yourself in this regard, to examine why it is that you seek the mission of helper. There is no shame in receiving external rewards—a good salary, recognition, status, even a "ticket to heaven."

Doing good is indeed the closest thing that mere mortals can ever do to be like God.

☐ Making a Difference

I am simplifying things considerably, portraying the motives as if each of us has only one that drives us. In truth, we are led by multiple urges. In the case of the woman above, for instance, who has devoted her life to helping others because it was the way she was raised by her aunt, that is not the complete picture. As an adult, she has also made certain choices to take the path she has followed, mostly as a result of obligations to help others of her oppressed race.

"There is a disproportionate amount of social ills plaguing the African-American community: gang violence, poverty, drugs, teen and preteen pregnancies, homicides, and suicides. As a consequence, there is so much work and service needed. When I help, I give to or give back to my family, community, and my country. I feel I'm making a difference, and that at some point in time, my contributions will help make things better for my children, for African-American children, for all children. As a consequence, by helping others, I would have contributed something to make the world better."

The desire to leave the world better off than when you arrived on the scene is among the most noble of human motives. So many people work in jobs in business, industry, sales, factories, law, where it isn't so clear to them—or others—that what they are doing is all that meaningful or socially redeeming. That is one reason such individuals choose to offer their help outside their normal careers.

I was backpacking in the wilderness of The Lost Coast, a remote region of Northern California that straddles the cliff faces of the ocean. Among my compadres was a man about my age who had recently retired from a career in business to devote himself to a lifelong dream of serving others as a "street lawyer," an attorney who works with the indigent.

"I had already done everything there was to do in my job. I made all the money I could possibly spend in my lifetime, or that of my children's lifetime. The work was no longer a challenge. And for 7 years I had this fantasy of going back to school to get a law degree so I could act as an advocate for those who have no voice."

Going to law school struck me as an unusual route to do good for others, especially since he was 25 years older than the other law students. I asked him about that as we continued to huff and puff up the next gorge, talking as much to distract ourselves from the pain of carrying 50-pound packs as to tell one another's story.

"Look," he said, slowing down his cadence so we could walk in a rhythm that would make it easier to converse. "I want to do something meaningful in my life other than making money. I want to help people, especially those who need it the most. I know that lawyers have a bad reputation." [He chuckles aloud] "Did you hear the joke about why lawyers . . . ?"

We distracted ourselves for a few minutes telling lawyer jokes, before we returned to the more serious subject that made him feel a little uneasy putting into words. "I guess my mother inspired me," he said pensively, warming to the subject. "I want to do the same for my own kids. I want them to see how important it is to give something back to the community. I want my daughter [He gestures ahead to where his youngest daughter is marching a hundred paces ahead of us] to see how important it is . . ."

He pauses for a moment, then continues. "No, that's not right. It's the other way around."

When I ask him what he means, he nods his head, as much to himself as to me. "Actually, it is my daughter who inspires me to do something good for others. I have listened to her, and watched her grow, all through her college years. She's had a big impact on me. I think I'm really following in her footprints rather than the other way around."

Lawyers sometimes have the reputation of being the most manipulative, self-serving, money-hungry professionals on the face of the earth. Yet here was a man who intended to use his training in law to do good for others. I realized that being a helper can take so many different paths other than the route with which I was most familiar. Furthermore, it is in the act of saving others that we also save ourselves.

Helping Others to Help Yourself

So far, from the voices you have heard, you might reasonably conclude that most helpers do what they do solely out of an altruistic spirit. The situation is actually a whole lot more complicated.

For one thing, as a beginner, you are likely to be far more self-conscious about what you are doing and why than someone who is more experienced in this work. The best helping is often the kind that seems automatic and effortless at the time. There is little or no conscious thought; it just seems like the thing to do.

When you read accounts of heroes who have risked their lives to save others, you often hear them say that they didn't think about what they were doing. Of course, if they *had* thought about it very long, they probably never would have done it.

The same often holds true for helpers in our line of work. "When I am being authentic," one counselor relates, "being who I truly am—which is not frequent—I just do what I do. And when I do what I do, then I do the most good. If that makes sense."

Actually, it doesn't make sense yet. But my guess is that she was just getting started.

"I am probably the best helper when I am not "on duty" as a helping professional. Maybe because when I have devoted so much time, so much education and training, and so much study to making myself the best helper, I have lost who I am in the process and my ego has taken over. I am now a "Helper with a capital H," who must exhibit certain characteristics and engage in certain behaviors, all of which comprise what scholarly research demonstrates as effective."

"I had a professor use a fabulous example of a centipede being asked exactly how it can walk like that with all those zillions of legs it has to coordinate at the same time. At that point, the centipede began to think about it and then it could no longer walk. As I sit here and think about why I help others, I can no longer do it in its most pure form. Do you know what I mean?"

This time, I know *exactly* what she is saying. In her words, it is the ego that sometimes gets in the way of our best work. Once we stop to think about actions, the flow of action stops altogether. When Csikszentmihalyi (1975, 1999) first coined the term "flow" to refer to the kind of effortless action that takes place when we totally immerse ourselves in action, he was interested in finding the essence of peak performance. In helping as well, we can enter the "zone," when we are "flowing," operating at optimal levels, doing our absolute best, all without thinking about our behavior or motives. Once we stop to consider what we are doing and why, the flow ceases.

I am not advocating that you shouldn't be self-reflective; quite the opposite, actually. I am just reminding you that although the helpers in this chapter, and the preceding one, act as if they truly understand why they are doing good for others, much of the time what we do is a mystery. We make something up to explain it after the events occurred. It is completely unacceptable to say to someone who asks you why you did what you did: "Gee, I don't know." Instead, we make something up, a reason that we hope will capture at least part of the picture.

The voices in the previous chapter make it sound as if the one motive they supplied describes the complete and total picture of what drives them to do good. The truth is a good deal more complex. It is certainly preferred to keep our egos out of the picture, to stay in a "flow" state in which our help is effortless and our motives are purely altruistic. While you can do this some of the time, it is inevitable that other, more personal needs will intrude. This is not necessarily a bad thing for which you should feel ashamed. It all depends on (a) the extent to which you are aware that you are meeting your own needs, (b) the amount of control these needs exert in your life, and (c) whether this is getting in the way of helping others (Corey & Corey, 1998).

Let's take it for granted that you want to make a difference in others' lives, that you feel the noble calling to relieve suffering and pain and to do your part to make your community a better place. Beyond this altruistic motive, there are often others of a far more personal nature that are mentioned.

☐ A Case in Point

We are well into the middle of a very intense discussion about what is in a client's best interests, when I hear this little whisper in the back of my head. It is annoying, distracting, breaking my concentration, so I try my best to ignore it. Until this point, I had been flowing, my ego completely harnessed, or so I believed.

I had been advocating pretty stridently that this person was wasting a lot of potential by continuing to work in a dead-end, menial job with no future. With the best of intentions I was urging her to consider doing so much more with her talent. Surely, there was no personal need I was meeting in this conversation. After all, what do I care what she chooses to do; it's her life, not mine.

Right.

The whisper started again, this time loud enough that it couldn't be ignored. "Who are you really talking to?" it asked me. I started to giggle. This reminded me of that Kevin Costner movie, *Field of Dreams*, when he hears that voice say, "Build it, and they will come," referring to the construction of a baseball field in a corn field. Then again, maybe I'm hallucinating.

Nah, I don't get let off that easy. This is a voice from my wiser self that just caught me trying to impose my values and will on someone else. Although it seemed as if I was looking out for only her best interests, the reality is that this woman was pretty content with her job situation; it seemed to bother me more than her. What was *that* all about?

Good question, huh?

What I wish to illustrate in this example is that so much of the time what we are doing, in the guise of helping others, is really designed to meet our own needs. This can be interpreted as *very* threatening, even offensive to some. Nevertheless, stick with me on this for a little longer.

Consider that everything we do is for a multitude of reasons. Some of these motives are within our awareness. Some are unconscious. Others we really know about, but pretend we don't. In any case, there are some very diverse and complex reasons why we do anything, especially making personal sacrifices for the sake of others we hardly know.

If you think about the reasons you want to help others, and if you are *really* honest with yourself, you don't have to look very far to find some self-serving motives. It makes you valued and important. It gives you a sense of potency and power, lets you feel in control. Maybe you like to help others so you don't have to think about your own problems; it is a good way to hide from yourself.

We are getting a little ahead of ourselves, though. Let's listen to what others have to say on the matter, at least a few who are willing to say out loud what so many others fear to admit to themselves.

☐ Giving and Receiving

"C. S. Lewis wrote years ago," a teacher tells me with authority, "that helping is a selfish act, especially when you are anonymous and don't want anything in return."

I am utterly puzzled by this statement and wonder where she is coming from, or what the heck Lewis meant. It seems to me that giving quietly, without fanfare or attention, is the ultimate in altruism since it is quite clear there is no ulterior motive.

She explains further: "Lewis argues that helping does more for the helper than the helpee and by making it anonymous you ensure that no one *can* reciprocate, emphasizing the intact and powerful nature of the helping gesture."

She can tell I'm not buying this and so quickly inserts, "I'm not quite this cynical. I think we need to help and be helped and that both take some practice in graciousness. Receiving help can be just as important. Lately I've been coming to the conclusion that we help most when it is natural, unconscious, and intuitive—when we don't actually set out to help someone but when we spontaneously give of ourselves or our time or whatever.

"People sometimes say I am helpful and kind and that puzzles me because I don't feel that I'm doing anything extraordinary and I know there are many opportunities to help that I overlook because I'm too preoccupied with my own stuff. But maybe that's not a bad thing. Maybe the best 'help' are simply the times when we are thoughtful, considerate, and respectful."

In other words, she is emphasizing that so often when we help we don't look at what the other person really needs but what we feel like giving. This is indeed selfish. It is also less than an ideal strategy for selecting the most effective interventions. It would be as if a physician decided to do a gall bladder operation on you, whether you need one or not, because she was in the mood to do one. This is not as absurd as it sounds.

I had a dentist friend who just returned from a training seminar on a new procedure for implanting teeth. While we were going for a long run together, he was telling me about how excited he was about this new technology and how anxious he was to try it out. Surely, I said to him in a kidding voice, he wasn't going to find a way to use this procedure with a patient today, whether he or she needed it or not. "Why not?" he replied, completely serious. "It's not like they wouldn't be getting a good service."

"Besides," he said after a short pause, "I need the practice."

At first I was appalled by this admission. My own teeth started to ache. But then I started thinking about how often I use favorite methods in my teaching or therapy, not because it is what my audience needs most, but because it is what I feel like doing at that moment. If you were to call me on this choice, I would of course have prepared some rationale to explain that my intuition, or best clinical judgment, leads me to make this choice of intervention. It would be closer to the truth, though, to admit that we all sometimes do what we feel like, whether it is in the best interests of the client or not.

Our effectiveness is dependent, in part, on our ability and willingness to suspend our own needs, to see clearly and accurately what a helping situation requires, and then to deliver that service. When we are functioning optimally, that is exactly what we do. There are times, however, when we ignore what is going on with a client and instead listen to our own preferences. Let me be clear that this is assuredly *not* sound helping practice. But that is not to say that it doesn't still go on, especially to the extent that we are not even aware of the ways we are meeting our own needs.

☐ Forget Your Troubles

Our field sometimes attracts people who have experienced great suffering or who prefer to get their counseling vicariously rather than directly. I suppose it is fair to say that we all have our problems and issues that we have not fully resolved. The key is whether you have gained enough awareness and insight into your issues that you can limit their effects on your work and transcend them to make yourself even more effective because you understand better the struggles that clients may have (R. E. Watts, personal communication, 1999).

As I mentioned before, more than a few helpers I've interviewed admitted, reluctantly at first, that they secretly enjoy working with people who are worse off than they are. It makes you feel better about your own life. The more you hear about other people who are struggling with problems far worse than your own, the better you feel.

I know helpers who carry a beeper and cell phone with them wherever they go and thrive on the interruptions they receive at all hours. Oh, they *act* annoyed when a call comes at an inopportune moment, but you can tell they really enjoy the feeling of being needed.

As long as you are focused on other people's problems, you don't have to think about your own troubles. You don't have to worry about the boredom or loneliness or lack of intimacy you sometimes feel. You can feel needed and important as long as others are so dependent on you for their welfare.

I am certainly not saying that most helpers choose this work as a form of distraction from their own problems. On the other hand, most of us would admit that there have been times when we are grateful for the diversion.

☐ Vicarious Living and Voyeurism

Many helpers talk about enjoying delving into the darker side of human existence—from a safe distance. You get to hear people's deepest, darkest secrets, their fantasies and fears. You have ready access to the most intimate details of someone's life; no question is out of line or too nosey. You have the opportunity to live a hundred, or a thousand, different lives with everyone you help.

A therapist in private practice identifies rather quickly that the reason he likes his work so much is because of the variety of experiences he can have by listening to his client's stories and accessing their lives:

"My life is really kinda boring, if you want to know the truth. I live according to routines and schedules, each hour segmented into its 50-minute intervals. I eat at the same places and order the same things. I do basically the same things day in and day out.

"In my work, though, it's a different story. I take only the most difficult cases, the more bizarre the better. It drives my supervisors crazy because I prefer working with those that everyone else tries to get rid of—the multiples and dissociative disorders in particular, the borderlines, whatever. I love listening to their stories. I love the drama of their lives. I love the complexity. I love hearing about all the shit they get into, and how they always seem to pull themselves out. I never watch television. Why would I ever want to? The stuff I see in my office is so much more interesting."

Another therapist I talked to turns away routine cases, finding them unchallenging and too predictable. "I like working with multiples, the more personalities the better." He has a gleam in his eye and is practically rubbing his hands together.

"If there isn't an opportunity for me to learn something new from a case, why bother?" he asks.

I hesitate to say that someone need not present severe pathology or distortion of reality in order to present special challenges. Personally, the cases that I have found the most difficult to deal with are the individuals who are most like me—those who intellectualize and hide behind words, those who are fast-talkers and therapy-wise, who know the rules of the game and how to get around them.

When I try to get through to these people, it's like I'm trying to get through to myself. When the sessions are over, I hear my own words reverberating inside my head, and I wonder who I was really talking to, them or me. That is one of the delights of this sort of work: We are constantly challenged to look at our own issues that parallel those we are trying to help.

I still love best the parts when I get to be very nosey and personal, asking the most intrusive questions, fully expecting honest answers. It is all in the spirit of being helpful, I tell patients, and I mean it, but I also relish the opportunities to ask about the areas that perplex me the most in my own life.

☐ Being Connected

The theme of feeling connected to others was mentioned in the preceding chapter, and it certainly deserves mention again because it plays such a significant part in this work. So often, helpers are the type who thrive on intimate relationships and often feel unsatisfied. After all, we are used to such a high level of sharing in our work, with our clients and colleagues. We are an emotionally sensitive and expressive group, by and large, fluent in the language of tears.

One therapist, who feels isolated and lonely some of the time, mentions how she really feels most alive when she is working.

"The unknown force has left a deep longing inside of me, a thirst that nothing else can quench, nothing other than that connection spiraling deeper and higher in each session with another human being who yearns to discover his or her higher purpose. Helping my clients discover that higher being buried inside of themselves is a joy that transcends the lightness of my own being. Connectedness breeds connectedness. My thirst is quenched, my isolation as a human being healed."

☐ Intimacy Without Rejection

Okay, this one is mine. No reason to disguise or hide anything. I enjoy helping because I like getting close to people, as close as anyone will ever get, but on my own terms. In earlier stages of my life, I was wounded terribly by rejection. As a teenager, the girls I liked never seemed to like me back, or at least in the way that I wanted. I walked around terrified to trust anyone deeply because I just knew that I would end up betrayed.

Sure enough, my worst fears were realized. The love of my life in college abruptly (or so it seemed to me) ended our relationship. I was despondent, even suicidal. I didn't think I'd ever recover, and maybe I never have. But I swore to myself, then and there, I wouldn't risk letting anyone hurt me like that again. Of course, that was a ridiculous promise to myself, one I have broken a hundred times over.

With my clients and students, however, I get to be the one in charge. I set the rules. I guide where we go. I reveal only as much as I want. Yet I enjoy extremely caring relationships with those I help. Furthermore, they are so grateful for what I offer. It is a perfect situation for me in many ways, although it also prevents me from developing more egalitarian friendships because I am so used to being the one in charge.

A counterpoint to this rather self-critical confession is offered by a nurse who notes that her personal relationships are consistently enhanced by her work: "The more I learn about relationships," she says, " the better I can relate to others in my personal life."

This theme is also articulated by a teacher who shares the belief that helping relationships only enhance personal ones.

"When being a helper is a way of being rather than doing, I think the benefit is best characterized as intimacy. I'm thinking of friends who have or have had breast cancer; when they are in the throes of chemo, I have a sense that they have our share of the disease, that in some sense, breast cancer is "our" disease. To the extent that we are able to walk through the horror of breast cancer together, we experience a level of intimacy that cannot be described, and that prevails after the cancer is gone. I celebrate life and friendship each time I think of one of these courageous women.

"To borrow from Carl Rogers, the experience of psychological contact is the most powerful thing I know. I think this notion captures the benefit I have derived most from my work, training, and desire to serve others.

"My former fifth grade students are now 35. I still am thrilled when I hear of their achievements. I still grieve when I know of their pain. I love to get letters from them. Memories of students who allowed me to accompany them on journeys through and out of hell simply create a visceral experience I cannot describe. When my graduate students experience a level of psychological contact with their clients and the lights begin to come on, I feel a resurgence of life and new level of psychological contact—pure intimacy."

I get so inspired when I read this teacher's words. They make me hungry to run out right this minute and find someone I can help, someone I can feel this close to. Then I remember that although my students and clients have taught me about this closeness, it is with my friends and family that I can most meaningfully practice what I have learned.

☐ Power and Control

I'm sure you are well aware that some people become helpers not because they want to assist others but because they enjoy the power they wield in pulling others' strings. If you are the sort of person who is powerless and insecure, who does not feel much in control over your life, who thrives on manipulating others, what better place to address your fears than sitting in the driver's seat?

This field attracts unscrupulous, manipulative, even sociopathic individuals who exploit others. Think about it: If you wanted to boost your self-esteem at the expense of taking others down a notch, can you think of a better job, except perhaps politics?

On a more pedestrian level, quite a number of helpers readily admit that they enjoy the power that comes from influencing others. Think about what a kick it is to have others hang on your words. Think about how important you feel knowing that others' lives depend on what you do. This is an awesome responsibility indeed, but one that makes us feel giddy.

☐ Being a Know-It-All

There is indeed a certain respect and wisdom that are enjoyed by those who help others. It is not just the look of appreciation in another's eyes that infuses us with a sense of personal power, but also the knowledge that accompanies genuine acts of compassion. This is one of the selfish payoffs that result from doing good, poetically described by Ram Das and Gorman (1985) in their reflections on the meaning of helping: "The reward, the real grace of conscious service, then, is the opportunity not only to help relieve suffering but to grow in wisdom, experience greater unity, and have a good time while we're doing it" (p. 16).

Ideally, humility would be coupled with true wisdom. There is no need to show off, to prove to others how smart and clever we are. Nevertheless, helpers feel tremendous poise and confidence knowing that they are privy to the secrets that are rarely spoken aloud.

☐ Learning to Love

One woman related the story of how taking care of a relative taught her a lot about the act of loving.

"I have an elderly uncle for whom I am responsible. For the past several years I have spent nearly all my vacation and sick time traveling the 600 miles to his home to take care of him. I once gave up my job entirely and moved in with him but that didn't last long for a number of reasons. He is currently in the hospital and soon to be transferred to a nursing home. He has had a fall, a stroke, a heart attack, pneumonia, and four separate blood infections. He suffers from dementia, thinks he has lots of money and leaves cash lying around. He's set his stove on fire twice and routinely eats food he's left out overnight or cooked too long. He alternately "loves" me or abuses me verbally.

"We were never close. I saw him maybe 6 or 7 times growing up. He didn't lavish me with gifts or step into my father's shoes when he died when I was just 7 years old. So I recently asked myself, as many others have asked me over the years, 'Why am I doing this? Why do I give so much to him when he gave so little to me?'

"My brother, who lives 400 miles closer to my uncle won't do anything and thinks I'm crazy to care. Then it dawned on me: This isn't about my uncle. It's about me, about the kind of person I want to be. So when I asked myself why God lets my uncle live this excruciating life, past all pleasure and comfort, I realized it's for me. For when he finally dies I will be a better person than I was before he ever needed me. I won't necessarily be smarter or richer but I will be better in a very essential way.

"I started caring for my uncle because I love my mother and he is her brother. But now I have learned to love him and value my role as his caregiver for what I have understood it to be: a gift to me.

"A side value of this is the empathy I now have with others I know who have recently buried brothers, parents, even grandparents and children. We all know the frustrations of dealing with the old, the trials of paperwork, the exhaustion, the expense. We know the push/pull of competing responsibilities and the scorn of others. And we know what is valuable in life, and we all know a little more not only about how to live, but how to die. My children will have an easier time caring for me because I cared for my uncle. And that is of great value to me. So I don't feel altruistic at all. For what I am getting out of this far exceeds what I am giving."

☐ Helping Too Much

The woman in the previous example talks very frankly about the fact that the caring she gives is just as much for herself as for her uncle: She needs to give. Sometimes this need gets in the way.

A supervisor of student teachers has the opportunity to watch the way that beginners are trying to find a balance between offering just the right amount of help that children need without exceeding what is in their best interests. She has noticed that so often teachers try to do too much for kids, without considering that they might be acting to reduce their own sense of discomfort and helplessness:

"Just this week a little boy I know had just returned to school after a 7-hour operation to remove a brain tumor. All his classmates were excited to have him back and wanted to help him all they could. The trouble was they tried to help too much! Everyone wanted a turn at pushing him around the place. This is fine except sometimes he doesn't want to be pushed around. Sometimes he just wants to spend time with his friends, not with *all* the class members who insist on their turn. The teacher thinks this is wonderful—she doesn't realize how he is feeling."

One of the lessons to be learned from the narratives in this chapter and the previous one is that the act of helping is both selfless and selfish behavior. We are doing it to relieve suffering, to make a difference in the world, to express love and caring, but also to meet our own needs. The really hard part of this paradox is to monitor yourself and your interventions carefully enough so that you don't confuse what your clients need with what you desire. It is okay to enjoy this work a lot, even to thrive on the personal benefits that result, but only after you are certain that every action you take is in the best interests of those who are in your care.

What Matters Most

Thus far, you have seen that people who choose to help others, either for a living or as an avocation, are obviously not in it for the money. There are far more lucrative professions, many of which offer greater prestige, status, power, and compensation. You have also seen how doing good for others results in doing good for ourselves in a number of ways that no other activity can quite touch.

One of the benefits of this type of work is that it encourages us to be discerning and inquisitive about the world, about people's behavior, and about why people do the things they do. Helping requires a degree of daily contemplation and reflection in which we try to make sense of the things we have heard and seen. We continuously scrutinize other people's motives and intentions, attempting to form hypotheses about how they got themselves into a mess and what they might do to get themselves out. As such, we are philosophers, scientists, and theoreticians. We form theories to explain and predict behavior. Most importantly, we develop a framework to guide our interventions.

In order to do good, we must have an idea about: (a) what we think the problem might be, (b) how the person ended up in this predicament, and (c) what it will take to make things better. Once those questions are answered, the next logical step is to formulate a plan for how to best reach the identified goals. In this chapter we will look at what helpers believe makes the most difference in their work, what they do that matters most. If you haven't already given this considerable thought, rest assured you will spend the remainder of your life trying to uncover the most potent ingredients that produce lasting change.

☐ Helping as a Two-Way Process

Helping is really about affecting people, whether that influence is offered in the form of support, caring, or more direct action. Furthermore, it is always a reciprocal act in which both parties are involved in the process. In other words, it isn't your sole responsibility to figure out what is wrong and how to fix it, but rather to act as a guide for others to find their own way.

A teacher in New Zealand tells the story of how she clarified her main role as a helper:

"I met Nigel in his first year as an undergraduate student in teacher education. He was a Māori man [indigenous New Zealander] of about 30 years, married with 5 children and a practicing Mormon. He had come from the freezing works [slaughterhouse] and had worked in the sewers of this industry. When I asked him what brought him to the university he told me that he was sitting in a sewer one day talking with the rats and he told these rats that he deserved something better than this. He did not want to spend the rest of his working life with rats for company. The rodents seemed to listen but were indifferent to his plans.

"Nigel's first year as a university student had many challenges but he quickly became adept at understanding the system, including what was required. To support his family he also had to work 6 nights a week at a bread factory, starting at 8.30 p.m. and getting home at 4.30 a.m. Sometimes he fell asleep in class, he was so exhausted.

"He had to write an essay for a course I taught, and it was not a good essay. I knew about his background and how hard he worked but I also knew that the essay was largely incoherent. I gave him a D. I felt pretty bad about grading it so low yet I knew I couldn't pass it given the criteria for the essay and what he had produced.

"I tried to soften the blow a little by giving extensive, constructive feedback on the essay to point out features he could improve. I know that sometimes this just aggravates students more. They feel it's rubbing salt in the wounds to give such detailed feedback.

"Anyway, I ran into Nigel later on in the carpark [parking lot] at work. His wife had just arrived in their van with the children to pick him up. She wore glasses and the end of them had been taped to hold a broken piece together. Nigel proudly introduced me to his wife as his teacher. I felt somewhat ashamed at his gracious introduction. After all, I was the lecturer who gave him a D. Then he said the most amazing thing. He told me how grateful he was for that D, how it had helped him enormously to see where he had gone wrong and how it had motivated him to do better. His wife also smiled and thanked me—it did Nigel so much good, she concurred. I didn't know what to say other than 'Oh.' After a few moments I collected myself and said how impressed I was with his attitude. Some students would not have reacted so positively—in fact, quite the opposite. His response showed what a great learner he was, seeing setbacks as learning opportunities.

"The sequel to this story is that Nigel and I remained in touch over the years and this year he graduated with his Masters degree—the first in his family to go to university let alone get a post-grad degree—and he's now lecturing in computer studies at a Polytechnic [community college] and has two more children! I was delighted to catch up with him at graduation, and as we hugged he thanked me again for what I had done for him. I felt that I had done so little and that *he* had done so much, yet I felt it was necessary to accept this compliment—his way of helping me to feel I do make a difference in some way."

☐ How Change Occurs

As you read this story, you will have formed your own impressions of what you think mattered most to this Māori man. Did the D grade get his attention, as he reported, and motivate him to work harder? Was the specific feedback he received on the paper most helpful in structuring his attempts to improve his writing skills? Maybe the changes he made had nothing whatsoever to do with the paper at all; perhaps it was the caring and supportive relationship he felt from his instructor that encouraged him. There are endless other possibilities as well, many of which may have been related to variables outside the classroom.

The interesting thing about dramatic change processes, such as those reported by Nigel and his instructor, are the different explanations that are possible to account for the progress. Nigel had in mind one theory to explain his turnaround. His instructor had not even been aware of his new resolve and didn't see any appreciable difference in his performance, at least while in her class. Even after the fact, if she were now to theorize about what happened, she would supply other reasons to account for his growth. And a dozen observers of this phenomenon might very well give their individual theories about what happened. It's complex and confusing, isn't it?

Ask any experienced helper to provide a theory to explain how he or she helps most and it's likely you will hear a well-developed framework. After all, this is a question that you will be asked a lot, by almost anyone who approaches you for assistance. They want to know what you think is going on and what you propose to do about it. After relief is in sight, then they will want to talk about what you believe happened. Even if they are not curious enough to pursue this line of inquiry, you will feel intensely interested in making sense of what occurs when you are a participant in the change process. If for no other reason, you need to know what you did, and what role you played, so you can duplicate similar successes in the future.

You would be well advised to do your own research on the subject, which means reading a lot and talking to many helpers. Most likely, every instructor and supervisor you encounter will have some rather strong ideas about the best ways to promote change in others. The frustrating part of this is that often their explanations will directly contradict one another. Some mentors and experienced helpers will say, in the strongest terms possible, that you should develop strong relationships with your clients, that this is where most of the action takes place. That sounds reasonable, except when you hear so many different conceptions about the best form that helping relationship should take. Then others will tell you that the relationship is incidental; what matters most are the opportunities you create for helping people to practice new behavior. Repeat that theory to someone else, and they will snicker, telling you to concentrate instead on challenging people's belief systems.

There are literally hundreds of different theories that you will encounter to help explain what matters most in the change process. Needless to say, this is *very* confusing, especially for a beginner who is only trying to get a handle on the basics.

As you sort through the possibilities of what you think might be going on with any change incident (you never really know for sure), as well as what you can do to be of service, consider the ways that people are most likely to change. Quite a lot has been written on this subject of change processes (see as examples: Bohart & Tallman, 1999; Curtis & Stricker, 1991; Hubble, Duncan, & Miller, 1999; Kanfer & Goldstein, 1986; Kottler, 1991, in press; Mahoney, 1991; Prochaska, DiClemente, & Norcross, 1992), trying to describe the complex ways that people are most permanently transformed by helping experiences.

In an effort to simplify matters, let's cut through the arguments about what is supposed to really promote change. If we look at what all the theories have in common, instead of how they differ, what we are left with are several variables that exert the most influence. Regardless of the setting in which you help, the population of folks you work with, and the particular approach you take, the following ingredients are likely to be present.

☐ Altered States of Consciousness

You have probably noticed that in some circumstances, you can talk to someone until you are blue in the face and you will have no impact whatsoever on them. In another context, with perhaps another individual, the person can hear the exact same thing, then turn around and act immediately. The differences, of course, are the credibility of the influencer and how skillfully the situation has been set up to capitalize on persuasion and the readiness of the person.

Hypnosis, for instance, is built upon the idea of helping people to become hypersuggestible to what is offered. During altered states of consciousness, when concentration is focused and expectations are controlled, apparently magical things can happen within a very short time. Most helping efforts occur in this context. The person in need of help is open to what is offered. He or she is in a perfect state of readiness. In order to have maximum impact, therefore, you want to set things up so that the person is attentive, eager, and open to what you are doing.

☐ Placebo Effects

This most simply means capitalizing on people's expectations. If you believe that what you are doing is going to be useful, and if you can convince the other person to share your conviction, then your help is far more likely to be successful. Your job, then, is to inspire hope. In one sense, you are a kind of faith healer who helps others to believe, with all their hearts, that deliverance is right around the corner (Fish, 1973; Frank, 1961).

The people who come to you are often apprehensive about the future. They feel lost or scared. They are anxious or depressed. Most of all, they sincerely wonder if anything will ever be different. They look to you for hope.

If you were really honest with people during the first moments of a helping interaction you would often have to admit that you don't have a clue about what is happening, nor do you have more than an inkling of an idea about what to do. That is not to say that you show any of this on your face. Quite the contrary, you act as if you are fully in control and as if you know *exactly* what you are doing. Granted, there are some helpers I know who say that they *do* know what is going on and where they are going from the start, but these reports are so different from my own experience they scare me. In any case, whether you feel confident or not, it is important that you appear that way. Other people are depending on you for support. They are looking to you for hope.

It isn't exactly lying when I tell people that I *know* I can help them, that I'm sure they've come to the right place. I can see the look of relief on their faces, so I know that the effects of my work are already operating: They are already changing just with the prospect of help on the way. I also know from experience that given enough time, I will be able to help the person figure out what is going on and find some satisfactory solutions to the problems he or she is facing. I may not yet know in the first meeting or two exactly what I'm doing, but I do have full confidence that eventually we will figure it out together.

Of course, you would not admit this aloud, just as you would not want to be privy to what your doctor is really thinking as she examines you or begins a procedure. Bill Cosby tells the story of having an operation. Just as he is about to go under the anesthesia and lose consciousness, he hears the surgeon say, "Oops." He immediately asks what happened in a state of panic, to which the doctor replies, "Nothing," unconvincingly. "Oops," is not the sort of thing you want to say out loud to someone you are helping. You want to present yourself as confident, poised, utterly in control of the situation. Sometimes, this very posture is enough to inspire sufficient hope in others that this is all it takes.

☐ Helping Relationship

All helping occurs within the context of a special kind of alliance that is built on trust and interpersonal influence (Hovarth & Symonds, 1991; Kottler, Sexton, & Whiston, 1994; Orlinsky & Howard, 1986). While some believe that this caring relationship is sufficient for change to occur, it is most definitely the glue that holds everything else together. If you do nothing else for someone (sometimes it feels like there really is so little you can do), you hold them in your arms, metaphorically speaking. You provide the kind of safe, caring, accepting, and loving environment that is so needed during times of great difficulty.

More than being a simple "holding environment" as this is sometimes called, you also put in place certain boundaries that help people to feel that things are in control. While they may occasionally test these boundaries (come late, bother you at home, attack your credibility), they are as much a part of what is considered therapeutic as any compassion that you exhibit.

In other words, not everyone needs the same kind of relationship. With one person, you will sense immediately that she is practically dying for a little understanding and compassion. With another person who may appear more dependent and needy, you will surmise that he is likely to respond much better to a relationship that is more structured.

As your helping relationship evolves, you will also notice that things must be managed quite differently in subsequent stages. In the beginning, you might present yourself as a confident and knowledgeable expert, later as warm and accessible, still later as more like a consultant than a teacher. It all depends on the particular client, the situation, the presenting problem, and the stage you are at in the relationship.

My son just went off to college for the first time, causing a very abrupt shift in our relationship. I am used to being responsible for certain things in his life—making his travel arrangements, for example, or reminding him to take care of certain tasks. Within a matter of hours of arriving on campus, I started to slip into the familiar pattern and then was curtly reminded that those services were no longer welcomed nor needed. I have my doubts about that, but it is altogether clear to me that we have entered a new stage in our relationship in which previous sorts of interactions are no longer effective or even appropriate with him.

I must now learn new ways of relating to my son, negotiate different boundaries. The power has shifted dramatically in terms of who now controls when and how we communicate. Unless I am prepared to adjust to this new stage, we are likely to be in for a very bumpy ride. As it is, all my grief and loss during this transition could cloud my judgment about what is most helpful to him at this stage in his life. As a therapist and teacher, however, I have had lots of practice in negotiating these altered norms for relationships. I have learned that one of the single most important helping skills is flexibility—going with the flow of what is needed.

Cathartic Processes

The helping relationship just described creates an atmosphere that is conducive for people to tell their stories and share their thoughts and feelings. People do often feel so much better when someone listens to them, reflects what is heard, and clarifies issues. Sometimes it is enough to just talk about what is most bothersome, even if there is nothing that can be done about it at the time. If you do nothing else for someone, if you can't intervene in a dramatic way, if you can't wipe out poverty or mental illness or cancer, you can still help him or her to feel understood. This is miraculous. It almost cannot be overstated how important this part of the helping process is, even if it might be insufficient by itself to promote necessary changes.

Listen to people. Very carefully. With compassion and caring. Let them know they have been heard and understood. Help them to tell their stories. Reflect back on the themes and issues that emerge. Generalize from this story to other aspects of life.

Consciousness Raising

This is just a fancy term for promoting insight or changing someone's mind. So often people feel stuck or helpless, not because of their life circumstances, but because of the way they are choosing to look at things. If you can introduce another way to perceive their situations, an alternative reality, the hopeless feelings can be lifted.

"You are stuck because you *believe* you are stuck," you might say to someone who has given up hope. "But if you are really not stuck at all, but merely temporarily in a rut, then you can do what it takes to get back on track."

Then you wait. Hold your breath. See if the person buys what you are selling. Sometimes, amazingly enough, pointing out this alternative perspective changes the whole tide of things. You can actually see the look of wonder on the person's face as he realizes that everything is now different, just by thinking about his situation in a different light.

There are as many different ways of promoting such insights as there are approaches to helping. Let's say that someone presents you with a situation in which she feels trapped in a marriage. "I'd like to be out on my own," she tells you, "but I just can't right now." When pressed further, she elaborates the reasons: "For one, I can't afford it. I have no money of my own, no way to earn a living. Then there are the kids; it would be awful for them. My husband would probably fall apart. Besides, I'd probably never be married to anyone again. Maybe it's better to stay in a lousy relationship like this."

That last statement was really expressed as an uncertain question of doubt. She is obviously struggling with whether to stay in the marriage or get out and you can tell in which direction she is leaning. She has lots of very good excuses for staying where she is.

If you were going to help this woman, offer something of value to her that might get her thinking in a constructive way, what would you say? Like so many such encounters, there are dozens of therapeutic options to raise her consciousness. Here are just a few possibilities.

- *Clarify her feelings*: "I really hear your ambivalence. A part of you would like to escape this marriage which doesn't meet your needs, but you also feel a lot of fear being out on your own."
- *Confront her excuses*: "When you say you can't afford to move out, that it would hurt the kids and all, what you really mean is that you prefer the misery you know rather than the unknown which could be worse."
- *Promote an examination of her story*: "I wonder where and how you learned to accept such mediocrity?"
- *Dispute those beliefs that appear illogical*: "Where is the evidence that these things you predict would, in fact, occur?
- *Use paradox*: "You are probably right. You really are trapped. There is no way out and no sense even trying."

This is just the smallest sampling of intervention choices, each of which is designed to get the person to think differently about things. Such insights can lead to dramatic changes when followed up with other efforts.

It isn't your job to spoon-feed people with your wisdom, nor to force them to accept conceptions that they don't want or feel ready for. One seasoned veteran explains how he has learned that sometimes doing less is doing more:

"To me, being a helper means freeing people up. It's a lot like planting a tree. You find a good location where there is plenty of sun, dig a big hole, put the tree in the ground, pack good soft dirt and fertilizer around it, and then get out of the way and let it grow. Every once in a while, check in and give it a little water."

This prescription for helping may sound a little simplistic, but it reminds this therapist about the dangers of working too hard on others' behalf. "I'm worried," he says further, "that too many people in the helping professions plant their trees and then every day pull them up to see how they are doing. They get too involved directly in their work with their clients."

Reinforcement

It isn't just behaviorists who systematically encourage people when they do things that are good for themselves. Every time someone you are trying to help does something that you think is constructive, you tell them so.

- "Atta boy!" a mother tells her son who just hit a perfect backhand after she changed the grip on his tennis racquet.
- "You must feel so proud," a teacher says to a student who just got his first A on an assignment.
- "That took so much courage to do that," a friend admits, "I don't think I could have done nearly as well."
- "I'd like to see that again," a social worker tells a young father who just tried a new discipline strategy.
- "Wow," a nurse exclaims to her recovering patient, "you're making such excellent progress on your exercises. The difference is startling."
- "Good job in reading that situation," a supervisor tells an employee after she has presented a difficult case.

In each of these instances, and a thousand others, the helper attempts to reward constructive behavior, knowing that reinforcement increases the likelihood that such actions will continue in the future.

Sometimes, we try to do so much more for people than they really need. As a parent, teacher, or any sort of helper, the hardest thing to do is stand on the sidelines, let others make their inevitable mistakes, and wait until they do something good that we can support. Sometimes, we have to bite our tongue because the wait takes a very long time.

Rehearsal

Given the safety and trust that are implicit in most helping relationships, there is an atmosphere established that is very conducive to practicing new behaviors. This can run the gambit from impromptu enactments to formal role plays.

- "So, tell me again what you're going to say to your husband when you get home."
- "I'd like to hear you say out loud what you're going to tell yourself the next time you get in that situation."
- "I'll be your mother. Talk to me just the way you intend to present your position."
- "You say you don't have the guts to confront anyone. How about confronting me right now with how angry you feel that I keep pushing you on this."
- "One more time. Let's see exactly how you're going to approach things."

The intent of any rehearsal strategy is to give people the opportunity to practice new behaviors, receive feedback on its effectiveness, and then fine-tune efforts before they are attempted in the outside world.

Task Facilitation

Going hand in hand with rehearsal during consultations is practicing the new strategy in real life. This can involve structured homework assignments or more casually declared goals that will be worked on between meetings. Talk is cheap, unless concerted attempts are made to put into action what was discussed.

- "I hear you saying that you want to be assertive in your life. So what exactly are you going to do, with whom, and when are you going to do it?"
- "You've been talking for some time about the need to diversify your life and become more involved in different activities. Let's talk about how you might do that."
- "That is the fifth time I've heard you say that you can't stand the way you are treated at work. So, what are you going to do about it?"
- "It might be helpful if you started keeping a journal to keep track of the times you feel most out of control, what works best, and what doesn't work at all."
- "You say that you and your girlfriend argue at least twice every day. This week, I'd like to see if you can increase the frequency to an average of three times each day."

This last assignment might sound comical but is actually an example of a "paradoxical" directive that is designed to be disobeyed, or at least to shake things up. When someone does not respond to direct suggestions, it is sometimes helpful to try the opposite (also known as "reverse psychology").

Your job as a helper, especially when you have limited contact with folks, is to spend your time in such a way that they can do the work outside of your sessions together. Even if you have a single conversation with someone, you can still use the time constructively to plan future intentions.

Major Demolition

Sometimes it takes a major shake-up in order to help someone break loose from old, dysfunctional patterns. I first thought of this idea (Kottler, 1991) while listening to a replay of the Apollo space mission when photographs were first sent back showing what Earth looked like. The whole world waited with baited breath but the expensive Hasselblad camera failed to work. After the engineers at Mission Control in Houston exhausted all their brilliant ideas for fixing the camera, one expert yelled to the astronauts in exasperation to "kick the damn thing." They did. And it worked.

This solution to the problem is not unlike what I've heard some psychiatrists say about the way that shock treatment works. It is kind of like kicking the neurological system, restarting it the way you would a computer that has frozen or is on the blink. And in a way, this is just what we do sometimes when we try to help people: We try to kick them, or shock them, or demolish their current dysfunctional reality in the hope that maybe when they regain their bearings, things will be better calibrated.

Sounds primitive, doesn't it? Maybe it is even cruel to compare attempts at helping people to giving them a swift kick in the rear, head, or wherever else they need momentum. Yet at times people do seem to need being shaken up a bit, confronted vigorously, or forced to bring their buried heads out of the sand.

Modeling

Last, but hardly least, this final therapeutic dimension I will mention has to do with the way you present yourself to others. It is not only what you do that matters most with those you help, but also your manner and presence. If you are calm, confident, poised, and reassuring, you tend to inspire trust in others. If you can exude in your style a certain degree of personal competence and power, others will admire you and try to imitate your behavior. If you can demonstrate in your own life the ways you want others to be, they are far more likely to follow your lead.

In one study of master practitioners nominated by their peers, it was discovered (or rather confirmed) that the most effective therapists were those who demonstrated certain qualities in addition to their clinical skills (Jennings & Skovholt, 1999). Such professionals were found to be reflective and self-aware individuals, especially open to critical feedback and learning from their mistakes. They have exceptional relational skills, value complexity and ambiguity, and exhibit emotional maturity and strong character. They are, in the words of Carl Rogers (1961), "fully functioning" or, according to Abraham Maslow (1970), "self-actualized." This means they are the sort of people to whom others would gravitate.

When I asked an award-winning teacher how she believes she makes the most difference in the lives of her students, she was at first stumped.

"Ask an easy one why don't you! Geez, I don't know. Just the other week I re-met a teacher who heard me speak about 6 years ago. She was at another talk I was giving about a totally different subject. Anyway, she came up to me and told me she was still using the method for teaching math that I had talked about years ago. I didn't even remember what she was talking about.

"Well, such a comment is always rather bewildering yet affirming. I'd like to think that being a teacher in a university enables me to influence the widest number of people—adults who will go on to work with learners of all ages for many years, in many settings, and maybe they will remember something I said or instigated or challenged them about.

"Two weeks ago a friend told me that he teaches with a young man whom I'd had here a number of years ago. This young man told my friend that I was inspirational because I actually modeled what I talked about. So I guess if you ask how we make the most difference I'd say it's when we teach in an engaging, credible, accessible, and meaningful way. And this can mean sharing our muck-ups and how it went wrong as well as our great successes—helping students to see the process of growth and change."

It is this last dimension of modeling that I want to address a little more closely. You may be under the assumption that what you *do* is the critical element in any attempt to serve people, but I'd like you to keep in mind that who you *are*, the way you present yourself, is equally important. In one study, Jennings and Skovholt (1999) found that master practitioners possess certain personal characteristics in addition to whatever clinical skills they might have. They are people who are curious and inquisitive, not only voracious readers, but passionately engaged with life. They are both emotionally receptive and responsive. They are good at intimacy, applying relationship skills in positive ways. Finally, because they are well aware of what they have to offer people, they are good at harnessing these qualities to be most influential.

If you wish to be helpful to others, this means that you must develop who you are as a person, as well as the training you receive in helping procedures and skills. I'm not saying that this is enough to be helpful because there are lots of confident, knowledgeable people walking around who don't have the gumption or ability to help others a whit. Likewise, there are others who have plenty of training and helping skills who compromise their influence considerably because they don't appear attractive and powerful to others.

☐ The Altruistic Personality

Research has been conducted with individuals who have risked their lives in dangerous situations. These are people who helped victims of accidents, donated their kidneys to strangers, or rescued Holocaust victims. Based on this research, there appears to be a kind of virtuous, altruistic personality that is more inclined toward acts of service (Bierhoff, Kiein, & Kramp, 1991; Jeffries, 1998; S. P. Oliner & Oliner, 1988; Van Hesteren, 1992). These are people who not only exhibit altruistic *behavior*, but also altruistic *intention*, meaning they held no expectation for personal reward (Galston, 1993). In many cases, they didn't even think what they did was in any way unusual or extraordinary (Monroe, 1991).

Among those qualities most apparent in someone with an altruistic personality, Jeffries (1998) found a marked lack of ego. They don't do what they do for attention, approval, or rewards of any kind. They prefer a temperate, moderate lifestyle, showing restraint and internal control. They also exhibit qualities of fortitude and persistence, sticking with their efforts when things get tough. They exude a sense of fairness and justice, a belief in what is morally right. Finally, they feel a great sense of charity toward others, which is often manifested in empathy.

Based upon her own interviews with individuals who donated their kidneys to strangers, gave their money away to the needy, volunteered their time to work in charitable causes, or even risked their lives to help people, Brehony (1999) found that most of them shared several personal characteristics:

1. They feel a sense of commonality and connection to other people. They feel responsible for all others because of a perception that we are all brothers and sisters.
2. They are humble and modest, seeing their gestures as quite ordinary rather than special in any way.
3. They tend to be optimistic and prefer to see the best in others. They give people the benefit of the doubt. They prefer to reframe even the most distressful situations in the most favorable light possible.

4. Rather that looking at acts of service as a favor they have performed, they see it is an honor and a privilege.
5. They feel good about themselves and are healthy and happy, and thus are more inclined to give to others.
6. Their altruistic behavior occurs without conscious thought. They do good because it is the right thing to do. When queried as to why they give of themselves, they often seem puzzled by the question; they are more curious about why someone would *not* do what they have done.

Brehony (1999) also found among her sample of altruists that they were not inclined to judge others because they might act differently in similar circumstances. They did not preach or try to make others like them (although the world would be far better off if they could bring over some converts). "Not one claimed any special enlightenment—a good rule of thumb is that anyone who claims to be specially enlightened probably isn't" (p. 186).

This should all be familiar to you, hopefully because you recognize that you possess many of these characteristics.

☐ What Makes the Difference?

When you put all of the dimensions of helping together, what we've got is a distinct impression that the process is both complex and simple. On one hand, it is nearly impossible to figure out what really matters most to people when they are in the throes of transformation. On the other hand, we have seen that there are indeed a few variables that consistently operate in almost anyone's change efforts. These dimensions transcend particular situations, whether the person is changing in therapy, the classroom, or a vacation; they also transcend most cultures.

A conflict mediator in New Zealand, himself of Mäori heritage, describes in his own language how he believes he helps people the most when they are trying to resolve difficulties.

"I believe I bring a Mäori cultural perspective to the mediation process. I provide a bicultural "face" to those people who are seeking assistance and are of the same ethnicity. We call it "kanohi ki te kanohi," or the presence of a Mäori with a Mäori person. The ability to speak the same Mäori language is also a bonus, for the initial connection to be made."

Regardless of who you are working with, it is critical to speak their "language." To the extent that you are willing and able to respect and honor someone's cultural identity, whether that is based primarily in their ethnicity, religion, gender, or sexual preference, you are far more likely to build the sort of trust you will need to help them in constructive ways.

The influence that you exert with others is based not only on the trust you develop, but also on your personal power. If you are seen as someone who has "mana" and "ihi," as the Mäori say, then you are a potent figure, one worth listening to and emulating.

Of course, power and influence do not surge in one direction only, but actually flow back and forth between all parties involved. As much as we would like to believe that we are the ones in control, guiding, if not actually determining, how the interactions can be most therapeutic, our clients are doing their best to affect us as well. They want to change our minds, to convince us that they are right, that they have been misunderstood, that others are really the ones at fault. In some circumstances, whether due to intentional or inadvertent effort on the part of clients, we pay dearly for this close contact with others who are suffering. Doing good for others often carries consequences, and not all of them are desirable.

6

CHAPTER

The Price Paid

The more time, energy, and commitment you devote to others' welfare, the less there is left over to take care of your own needs. Sometimes this personal depletion happens inadvertently, the result of neglect and chronic work in the trenches without adequate time for recovery (Belson, 1992; Maslach, 1982; Sussman, 1995). Other individuals "hide" in their work as a way to avoid dealing with their own personal issues—the emptiness, loneliness, anxiety, or boredom they might experience (Kottler, 1993). In both cases, unless you are able to balance the amount of passion and commitment you devote to helping others with attention to your own needs, you will not be able to do much good for very long (Corey & Corey, 1998; Guy, 1987; Kottler, 1999).

Being a professional helper thus carries a number of burdens and responsibilities that lead to stress, burnout, and personal depletion. Volunteer helpers, as well, experience similar problems, plus additional ones that are unique to their chosen service. AIDS volunteers, for example, must not only contend with the stress of working with people who are seriously ill, but they also suffer stigmatization and are "socially punished" for their good deeds (Snyder, Omoto, & Crain, 1999).

Although thus far we have been examining the joys and satisfactions that helpers experience as a result of their work, it is also important to look at the sacrifices that are made along this path. Too often, people enter this field without complete "informed consent," that is, without being fully aware of the side effects and personal consequences that may occur as a result of helping.

Jean de la Bruyere (1688), a 17th century French writer, noted that there are inevitable costs and a certain amount of pain that comes with the territory of helping others: "That man is good who does good to others; if he suffers on account of the good he does, he is very good; if he suffers at the hands of those to whom he has done good, then his goodness is so great that it could be enhanced only by greater sufferings; and if he should die at their hands, his virtue can go no further: it is heroic, it is perfect."

It will probably not cost you your life to do good for others, but you will likely undergo your share of suffering as a result of your passion and commitment toward service.

☐ When Empathy Hurts Too Much

Compassion fatigue is a kind of "secondary" post-traumatic stress in which the helper suffers pain resulting from proximity to others who have been harmed. As Figley (1995) has pointed out, one can even develop symptoms just *hearing about* someone else's misfortune. I once lost a week's sleep after listening to the story of a colleague who worked himself to death, suffering a heart attack while on the job with his insane hours.

Breggin (1997) calls it "malignant empathy" when suffering becomes contagious. There is a kind of reciprocal influence that takes place between helpers and clients, for better and worse. While it is certainly the case that we learn a lot from those we help and feel inspired by their courage, we also "catch" their suffering. When you get too close to someone who is in the depths of despair, who is suicidally despondent, or who is unusually toxic, it is very difficult to come away from the encounter unscathed. Even the most experienced veterans get caught in the emotional hurricane.

One therapist describes what happened when she got a little too close to the flame:

"While driving home from the session, my legs shook violently. I just left my office from an intake interview with a new client. During the first half of the time, the new client, an actress, flooded me with the emotional details of her life, all in the most dramatic fashion imaginable. I felt like I was on a roller coaster listening to her, not quite sure what parts of what she was telling me were real and which were the result of her overactive imagination. I felt lost in the details and agitated by her bottomless anger."

The therapist stops to draw a breath and compose herself before she continues. It is clear that this incident still bothers her after so much time has elapsed.

"The actress rose from the chair and began prowling the room, as if she was on a stage, which maybe she imagined she was. At one point, when she swept toward the door, I feared that she was going to walk out of the session. I remembered thinking to myself that maybe that wouldn't be such a bad idea. I was feeling some doubts about whether I could help her. I wasn't sure I even liked her, and I didn't know if that would matter or not.

"Once the session ended, I decided that I would do my best to find a piece of her that I could break through and connect to even though this had been our first encounter. I felt a deep tranquility inside myself the way things had ended. Yet on my way home I trembled. I felt I had walked across a mine field and came out intact. I knew I had not totally passed the test yet. There is no easy journey for both parties on this road we travel."

What this therapist is describing is the collapse of boundaries that sometimes occurs when we allow ourselves to get too close to those we help. That is one reason that the earliest practitioners of therapy felt it was so important to keep a distance from clients, not only to further the transference but to protect oneself. This is a mistake that beginners make a lot. On the one hand, you want to present yourself to others as being as compassionate and empathic as possible, open and accessible, kind and caring, loving and considerate. Yet if you get too close, you can get eaten alive.

On the other hand, if you put too much distance between yourself and others, trying to be objective, to keep boundaries in place, to demonstrate professional detachment, you risk appearing withdrawn and cold. The key, then, is to find and maintain the appropriate distance in your helping relationships so that you come across as warm and inviting, yet you are able to create an atmosphere that is consistent and protects both of you from getting hurt. This is much harder to do than it sounds: It is so easy to get sucked into the client's "stuff." Likewise, it is tempting to distance yourself to the point where there is no real connection between you. To complicate matters further, every helping relationship needs to be constructed a little differently, taking into account the client's personality, symptoms, interactive style, and particular needs, as well as the stage of the process in which you are currently working. You may find it necessary to include a more structured relationship in the beginning of your helping efforts, loosening the boundaries as things evolve. All of these demands create a lot of stress for you to manage.

☐ Let's Talk About Stress

Helpers are experts at assisting others in reducing the stress in their lives. Although designed as an adaptive function in the body to respond to critical situations by mobilizing resources needed to deal with dangerous situations, in its chronic form stress contributes to a host of problems including viral infections, coronary disease, immune breakdowns, and ulcers, not to mention emotional impairment. Most interesting of all, it is a self-inflicted condition caused by the perception of threatening situations (Kalb & Rogers, 1999).

A number of symptoms of stress are already familiar to you. When experienced as part of your helping role, whether called secondary trauma (Carbonell & Figley, 1996), compassion fatigue (Figley, 1995), burnout (Freudenberger, 1975; Maslach, 1982), vicarious traumatization (Pearlman & Saakvitne, 1995), or countertransference (J. P. Wilson & Lindy, 1994), it is characterized by several symptoms (see Table 1) that can wreak havoc in so many ways and in so many personal domains (Yassen, 1995).

In its immediate state, stress is really just the "fight or flight" reflex that prepares the organism to do battle or to flee. Every system in the body makes necessary adjustments that increase specialized functioning: Digestion shuts down since it won't be needed (symptoms of dry mouth, fluttery stomach); the endocrine glands produce extra hormones that increase strength and speed (symptoms of tremors); lungs take in more oxygen to supply muscles with needed energy (symptoms of pounding heart and shortened breath); even hair stands at attention, making you look bigger and more formidable.

As a delayed reaction, certain side effects are also felt after stress reactions. The brain, adrenal glands, immune system, and liver are all activated to restore the organism to normal functioning once again. This restabilization and replenishment process also takes its toll on the body.

Finally, when stress becomes chronic because it is activated too often, serious problems result. Sleep and eating are disrupted. Fatigue and energy loss are common. Cognitive ability and memory are affected. Immune systems are diminished, making the person more vulnerable to disease and illness. For all of these reasons, many of your efforts to help people, whether to recover from disaster, illness, trauma, or life adjustments, will involve some

TABLE 1. Symptoms of helper stress (adapted from Yassen, 1995)

Cognitive	Emotional	Behavioral	Physical
Confusion	Depression	Withdrawal	Headaches
Difficulty concentrating	Sadness	Isolation from family and friends	Self-medications
Recurrent negative images	Guilt and self-blame	Nightmares	Sleep disruptions
Memory deficits	Hopelessness	Impatience	Somatic reactions
Irrational thoughts	Anxiety	Inappropriate risk-taking	Weight gain or loss
Loss of meaning	Numbness or emptiness	Repeated accidents	Lowered resistance
Perfectionism	Overwhelmed	Moodiness	Aches and pains

sort of stress reaction. It is interesting, however, to look at the stress in your own life as well.

"It does make me more than a little—make that a lot—anxious when I'm around people who are feeling stressed out," says one individual who does traumatic stress debriefings. These programs are designed to help rescue personnel recover from the effects of emergency work.

"On the outside, I appear calm and unflappable, because that's what these people need to see. They've already seen dead bodies and hysterical people screaming and crying and grieving. They might have been covered in blood. So I help them to process it all, and I do that by taking everything in stride.

"Inside, though, I'm churning. I mean, how can you hear these stories about death, mutilation, traumatic injury, and disaster without being affected? Some of these macho guys—firemen, EMS workers, cops—break down. That is almost as hard to watch as the original traumas!

"Then, while all this is going on, a part of me is thinking about my own life. Just like everyone else, I've got bills to pay, kids to raise, problems at home, and all that. No wonder I don't sleep very well."

Among the sacrifices you will make as part of your commitment to doing good for others, increasing your own stress level is a likely toll that will be paid. You will be haunted by nightmares about those you couldn't help, and many who you did help. You will hear their stories echoing over and over again in your brain, unable to shut the voices out. You will be subjected to manipulation and toxic games by those you help as a way to keep you from getting too close. You will spend lots of time with people who are so anxious or depressed they can barely keep themselves alive. Do you think after a little while, some of this might seep inside you and pollute your soul? Do you think you will escape unscathed? Do you really think you will go on about your life as if everything is perfectly okay when you know the extent to which others are suffering?

☐ Sources of Stress

The sources of stress in a helper's life can originate from several places including the work environment, the clients you see, and specific events, but it can also be self-induced. Taking these one at a time, let's begin with the job setting in which you offer your services.

Environmental Stress

Alas, the world would indeed be a wonderful place if people practiced what they taught to others, if they were as caring and considerate with their colleagues as they are supposed to be with their clients. Unfortunately, many settings in which you might work turn out to be infested with political intrigue, backbiting, scapegoating, and undermining. In other words, some people who devote their lives to doing good for others don't often treat those with whom they work as compassionately and considerately as you might expect. In some cases, the work environment itself can be downright toxic. Staff members can be very mean to one another.

In addition to the stresses you may experience as a result of working with colleagues (or supervisors) who are less than considerate in their interactions, you will face other obstacles that are part of the organizational system. Paperwork may drown you in tedium. The organization that you work for may be so unwieldy, chaotic, impersonal, and poorly run that any helping efforts seem diminished or sabotaged. Your caseload may be so huge and the need for your services so overwhelming, that any effort you make seems like an insignificant gesture. Your resources may be so limited that you are working at one quarter efficiency. The rules and restrictions on your activities so limit what you can do that you seriously wonder if the effort really matters.

Unfortunately, the circumstances just mentioned are so common that it is senseless to complain about them. Helpers get together and swap "war stories," competing with one another over who is most overworked and unappreciated. Unless you can change the system, it is a waste of time to complain about things you can do little about. The fastest way to increase your stress level, and ensure that you will have a very brief career, is to think about all these obstacles, annoyances, and restrictions that limit your efforts. Helpers who flourish do the best they can with what they've got. Rather than whining and complaining, they concentrate on what is within their power to change.

"I work in a school," a counselor confides in a hushed voice so the assistant principal in the next office doesn't hear, "where they don't value much what I do." She shakes her head, not in discouragement, but rather in amusement, and then continues:

"They try to overload me with administrative stuff to do—scheduling, hall duty, evaluation forms, discipline problems, all the things that the teachers don't have time to do, and the administrators don't want to do. If I thought about it, this could drive me nuts.

Some of the other counselors in the district have given up. They just do what they're told. Others try to buck the system, but they end up paying for the rebellion in one way or the other. But what I try to do is help people when and where I can. Sometimes it's a teacher who's upset, or maybe a parent who's angry about something; lots of times it's kids. Occasionally, even one of the administrators comes in to dump things out. They don't know what I'm doing as long as I keep the paperwork flowing. I just can't let all this stuff get to me or I'll end up a crouton."

I look at her quizzically. "Crouton," she says again with a smile. "You know, like toast."

Sure, I know *exactly* what she means. Every job I have ever worked at, whether as a volunteer, a consultant, an employee, supervisor, or regular staff member, had its share of annoying impediments to doing my work the way I thought it should be done to maximize benefits for others. It has taken me a long time to learn that this is the nature of human organizations, for better or worse. It is just one of the sacrifices we make that come with the job. Complain, if you like. Feel sorry for yourself, if you insist. Whine, if you can find anyone to listen. Mutter to yourself and feel resentful. But if you are truly serious about helping others, you will likely pay a small price in terms of environmental dysfunction. It is not usually that big of a deal ... unless you make it so.

Client Stress

Helpers spend a disproportionate amount of their time and energy thinking about a very few individuals who give them trouble. These are the ones who don't cooperate with your plans, who are resistant, angry, manipulative, or even dangerous (Kottler, 1992, 1999).

Remember that it is very difficult to get close to people, especially those who are suffering, without being profoundly affected by their struggles. Double this effect when the person is deliberately trying to get underneath your skin because you are perceived as threatening.

I once supervised a student who was having lots of trouble associated with a chronic illness. The physical symptoms must have been excruciating, and the medications he was taking made his daily struggles so much worse. I felt terrible for this young man, so much so that I gave him more than the usual latitude in completing his assignments on time.

I spent a lot of time thinking about this man and his predicament. I became afraid of my own mortality. I allowed him, in the words of one "12-step" program, to live "rent-free" inside my head. And yet the more caring I showed, the more he pushed me away. In fact, rather than appreciating my concern, he became rather hostile to me. As badly as I wanted to be helpful to him, whatever I tried seemed to make things worse between us. It was clear that he neither trusted nor liked me, a situation I couldn't help but personalize too much.

As if I didn't already have enough to do in my life, I thought about this young man during various times of my day. I caution students and beginning helpers not to worry excessively about their clients. I tell them that since such cognitive activity doesn't really help them, then it must serve some distracting function in preventing them from dealing with their own problems. Yet here I was almost immobilized internally because I couldn't find a way to reach this person, much less do much to help him.

I wish this story had a happy ending. Even after so much time has elapsed, I still think about him, still feel badly for him, and even worse for myself. I know that he was an angry and distraught young man who had a right to be scared. He also didn't have to like me or want my help. But I still feel powerless to let him go. I still wonder what I could have done to have had a more beneficial impact on him.

Keep in mind that this is only one of the thousands, make that tens of thousands, of people I have tried to help. I certainly can't remember all their faces and names, but a great many of them still live as ghosts inside my head and heart. They haunt me. I wish I didn't care so much, but then I think it might be worse if I didn't care at all. I feel noble in my regrets.

No matter how hard you try, how you try to insulate yourself, how you attempt to objectify things or depersonalize helping situations, how much supervision you get to keep things in perspective, you will still be deeply affected by certain clients. Imagine, for example, some of the following cases that may find their way to you.

- A 78-year-old woman is depressed and despondent. She seems to have all her faculties and cognitive capacities, yet she seems listless. As you get into her life story, you discover that she is a survivor of the Holocaust, having spent her childhood in concentration camps. She watched her parents and siblings die and everything she ever loved taken away. Now, 60 years later, all the memories that she tried to keep under wraps come flooding out. You are the one who will hear her story, in all its gruesome detail.
- A 14-year-old boy is thinking about killing himself. He knows where his father keeps a loaded gun and has given considerable thought to just where he would place the barrel (in his right ear).
- An old man, or rather a relatively young man who looks much older than his stated age, has given up hope. He is homeless and can't find work, even though he once had a thriving career. His children won't speak to him. He is hungry and tired. He doesn't know where to go next.
- A woman is a victim of a vicious assault. Her face has been disfigured and several limbs broken. All her sense of personal safety has been shattered. She can no longer stand being alone, even for a few moments.
- A 16-year-old boy has been told he is dying of leukemia, with only a few months left to live. He has four younger siblings who he takes care of since his parents abandoned them several years previously.

- Someone about your age, who looks like you and holds your basic values, is feeling that life is boring and meaningless. Everything seems predictable and routine. There seem few new challenges along the horizon.

These are just the individuals who inadvertently "penetrate" you. What about the ones who do so intentionally and maliciously?

It is highly likely that at some point in your work you will encounter folks who will do their best to make your life as miserable as possible. I wouldn't take this personally; it often isn't about you at all, but rather represents a consistently dysfunctional coping style, or sometimes an attempt to keep you at a safe distance.

Some of the clients most consistently mentioned by helpers as particularly challenging include the following.

- *The seductive individual who seeks to corrupt you or knock you off your pedestal.* One minister, for example, encounters quite a few members of his congregation who consistently vie for attention by acting in an inappropriately seductive manner. "I'm not a very attractive man," he admits sheepishly, "so I know they are responding more to my position than to me as a person."
- *The angry or hostile person.* In the most overt form, you will be ridiculed, screamed at, or otherwise abused through intimidation. This may occur for a number of reasons, such as the person's consistently aggressive style or maybe even an extreme reaction to something that you triggered. In any case, it is extremely stressful to be yelled at or abused by anyone, no matter how out of control they feel.
- *The manipulative or controlling person.* Lots of people will play games with you. They will shade the truth, or outright lie. They will study you closely, assess what bothers you most, and then literally stay up late at night figuring out ways to get underneath your skin. It is not that such individuals are evil (although some might not be very nice people), but rather that you provide a juicy target for their wrath. Perhaps you represent an authority figure they despise or remind them of someone who has hurt them in the past. Just as often, some people go through life getting their needs met through control of others. You would be no exception.
- *Someone in the depths of despair.* It is very difficult to be with those who are so depressed that they have lost all hope. They may be suicidal to the point that impending action is forthcoming. Even if they are not in immediate danger of hurting themselves (or someone else), they still feel so lousy that their mood becomes contagious. You may even be seeing this person because everyone else in his or her world has lost patience.
- *Those who find it difficult to listen and respond.* In order to help someone, he or she must be able to hear what you have to say, to take in your offerings,

and then to take some action. For a variety of reasons including cognitive deficits, underlying neurological conditions, or just plain distractibility, some people you will try to help just won't listen.

This is just the smallest sampling of the types of people many helpers find especially annoying or stressful to work with. When you lose your perspective, overpersonalize things, or experience strong countertransference reactions, your own stress level can even exceed that of those you are trying to help.

Event Stress

You do have a life of your own, complete with its own adjustments, transitions, crises, conflicts, and challenges. When things are going wrong in your personal life, there is often leakage into your helping work. If you are experiencing relationship, financial, or health problems, for instance, that could definitely create higher stress levels.

Watch carefully how the effects of your work are affecting your personal life, and vice versa. You can easily imagine how dealing with traumatic situations can seep into your family and social time. Likewise, when you are feeling anxious, upset, or depressed about something, such feelings can compromise your efforts to be helpful to others.

A law student, who volunteers his free time working for the Make-a-Wish Foundation to aid sick children, discloses that he does this sort of thing well only when he feels in control of his life. "It takes a degree of poise and confidence to get important people on the phone to ask them for favors. Even though I'm not doing this for myself, I still don't push people as hard as I need to—you have to be persistent in this job—when I feel weak inside."

Self-Induced Stress

It could be said that almost all stress is self-induced since there is a certain amount of perceptual interpretation involved. Stress is a name for something that you are telling yourself is dangerous or frightening, often way out of proportion to reality. It results from beliefs that may be exaggerated or distorted.

There are certain types of personality style that seem to predispose a helper to more than his or her fair share of stress. In one classic study of who is bound for burnout, Maslach (1982) found that those who have the following characteristics tend to be more vulnerable: submissiveness, passivity, impatience, intolerance, low frustration tolerance, conventionality, poor

TABLE 2.

Before	After
It's my fault this person didn't improve.	I did what I could. The rest is up to him.
I'm a lousy helper because . . .	I sometimes don't perform as well as I'd prefer.
I blew it completely.	I made a mistake, which is not surprising considering I'm human.
I don't know what I'm doing.	I don't know as much as I hope to know some day.
This is *terrible* that . . .	This is *unfortunate* that . . .
I must do this perfectly.	I'm a beginner at this so of course I will be less than perfect.

self-confidence. In other words, the way to prevent stress from getting the best of you is to be proactive and poised in the face of inevitable obstacles and challenges.

Helpers often exacerbate their own stress levels by holding expectations for what they can do that are way off the scale. They think they can "save" people single-handedly. They believe that when things don't go as expected it is all their fault. They blame themselves for acting less than perfectly in any situation. They are filled with doubt and fearful of the next failure.

Most of what can be done to manage stress levels involves talking to yourself differently, just as you might teach your clients to do. This style of intervention, often referred to as cognitive therapy (Beck, 1995) or rational-emotive-behavior therapy (Ellis, 1995) takes the form of identifying your distorted, irrational beliefs, and then substituting others that are more grounded in reality. Note in Table 2 how initial internal statements can be changed to those that are a lot more healthy and rational.

These examples highlight the ways that stress can be reduced by talking to yourself differently, that is, by changing your perceptions of what is going on. Just as you will do this a lot with your clients who are torturing themselves with faulty thinking, you can apply these same skills to your own irrational beliefs.

☐ What Helpers Have To Say

The preceding sources of stress provide a general framework for understanding and anticipating what is most likely to get in your way when trying to do good for others. Consistent with the theme of this book—looking at the experience of helping from the perspective of those who do this work—a number of practitioners mentioned several other, more specific ways that they get themselves in trouble.

Caring Too Much

Falling under the category of self-inflicted difficulty, it is not uncommon that you may find yourself caring a little too much for those you try to help. No matter how much you try to compartmentalize things, put distance between yourself and others, you may still feel yourself drawn into their lives to the point where you are profoundly affected.

Sometimes, the overcommitment and overinvolvement is extended less to any individual and more to a program that you feel invested in. A director built a training program from scratch. It was her baby and she fought tooth and nail to keep it running in the face of many obstacles:

"I have had to sacrifice a lot, in terms of time spent and worries created. I have been yelled at in lots of meetings. I was really humiliated here as I was fighting for the program in times of cutbacks. At the same time, some staff members tried to sabotage the program. In normal circumstances, I would have quit, but I knew that if I had, the program would have been closed. This meant that I had much less pay than I would have been able to get elsewhere. I spent a period of 2 or 3 years when I constantly thought about quitting. On top of this, I have been working on a Ph.D. thesis. It is all too much for me."

This administrator is indeed paying a dear price for her level of commitment and caring, yet she has no regrets. She fully realizes what she has given up and what she is sacrificing, and she knows that this has been necessary in order to keep her program going. Looking at things through her eyes, it isn't that she has cared too much, but rather that someone had to care enough.

Depletion

Another program administrator has suffered his own forms of stress in his professional life, giving up his free time, putting family and friends on hold, in order to do the kind of job that be believes deserves to be done. "It isn't that there is nobody else who could do the job," he says, "they just couldn't do it as well as I can."

He says this with perfect candor and modesty, not bragging at all. It is most likely true that he is the best qualified and most highly skilled administrator within his organization. Everyone else seems to realize this as well, so every time he tries to extricate himself from more responsibilities, he finds himself persuaded that only he can carry the torch. Not surprisingly, after years of this, he feels emotionally and physically depleted.

"There's lots of stress as I try to find ways to give more to people who want a part of me. I have enough to do that it would take three of me and I still couldn't catch up. It's hard for me to decide on priorities of where to give, how much, when, and to whom. Making the stress even worse is the decision of how much time and energy do I give to myself when I could be giving it to deserving others. All these pressures have hurt me and the significant people in my life."

He says this with genuine regret, yet when pressed as to whether he would have done anything differently, admits that he would not. "I'm proud of the work I've done," he says, "even though it has been so hard."

Spread Too Thin

From the previous two narratives it seems apparent that helpers are plagued with the temptation to take on far more work than they can reasonably do without affecting their health. Sometimes, it is the nature of the job to require far more from any individual than can possibly be delivered.

A new professor feels caught between the demands of her employer that lead to tenure and promotion and those service commitments she feels in her heart. She says with frustration: "The major focus of my job is doing research. Doing service of some kind is suicidal for my career. However, it would be betrayal of all that I have been taught as an African American to ignore my community's needs.

"Too often, I find myself overloaded, fatigued, and burned out with duties such as community activities, involvement, and mentoring and advocating for African Americans. Even though this work is not valued very much by my colleagues, I can't just pursue my career without concern for others who need me.

"The African-American culture adheres to the biblical scripture that says 'To whom much is given, much is required' or 'He who has much, owes much.'"

This professor believes deeply in the work she is doing, even though she is spread so thin she can't stay on top of all her other responsibilities.

Being Labeled a Bitch

Sometimes helping involves making tough decisions and doing what is right, even though others might not like it. You may even be resented for your efforts, or called names, because others are not happy with what you've done. I think over time, some of the people I have helped the most hated my guts and resented the heck out of me during our interaction. Likewise, some of my clients who liked me best didn't change much at all.

A woman who volunteers her time for many community organizations observes that the greatest sacrifices she has made are very personal ones. "When I became the first woman commissioner of our local baseball league, I realized that the difficult part of the job was not making hard decisions. The hard part was watching my reputation of being a nice, easy-going person transform into the image of being a bitch. Worse yet, this wasn't in the eyes of strangers but many who I thought were my friends. I am certain that, had I been a man, I would have been perceived as a great commissioner, fair and honest. But because I was a woman, I received the label 'bitch' instead."

Oversensitivity

Compassion and empathy can't exactly be turned off at will. There are times when all the heightened sensitivity you have developed, all the training and experience, make you vulnerable to others' suffering. During such times, it is hard to stand by and just ignore what is going on.

I walk through a supermarket, minding my own business, trying to find the refried beans in the maze of aisles, when I hear a mother screaming at her two young children who are doing nothing more than being kids. I look around me and see that nobody else seems to take notice of this interaction that hurts me deeply to witness. I have to forcibly pull myself away to avoid intervening.

Later that same evening I am in a movie theater waiting for the film to start. I want to block my ears but I can't help but overhear the conversation of the couple in front of me. The wife is nagging her husband because she doesn't think he spends enough time at home. The husband tells her to mind her own business and they bicker back and forth. I am dying to lean over the seat and tell them to behave themselves, or at least to help them to listen to one another. I look around me and nobody else seems to notice or care about this fight. Why can't I turn this sensitivity off?

As a beginner who is first learning helping skills, you will be even more conscious of the ways that other people behave. You will hear dysfunctional communication styles everywhere you turn. You will notice things that previously have been invisible to your untrained eye. Even within your own family and friends, you begin to notice things that make you feel very uneasy. At times, you will long for the days when you were innocent and unaware.

Taking Things Personally

Another sort of oversensitivity is the type helpers feel when they commit so much of themselves to the outcome of their efforts. You will hear a lot from peers, instructors, and supervisors about how important it is to remember that there is only so much you can do; the rest is up to the client, to Nature, to fate, to God, or to factors outside of your control. Furthermore, sometimes you can do your job absolutely perfectly, far better than anyone else could have done, and you will still experience failure.

Looking back on her career as a nurse and then a therapist, one practitioner talks about how she takes things a little too personally.

"In nursing, because I chose an area—renal failure—I had these long-term relationships with my patients. Either they were on dialysis or they had a transplant and had to visit the clinic to be monitored for the rest of their lives. That meant I spent a lot of time with these people. But it also meant that they died a lot and I felt very sad. I went to a lot of funerals in my 8 years as a nurse, and it never got easier.

"When I began having recurring nightmares, I had to leave. I wouldn't trade those 8 years, or the quality of those relationships, but it was like a lifetime of losing friends telescoped into a brief period without a whole lot of time to recover in between.

"Now that I'm a therapist, I use myself even more in my work. It's more personal because I use more of my own process. When people don't get better now, it feels like even more of a personal failure; I can't blame their disease."

It feels so much more personal to her because in this work there really is so much more personal involvement. The boundaries we put in place are more illusionary than real. And as she explains further, you can never do enough preparation to insulate yourself from the power of these helping experiences.

"It's not a question of needing a better manual, or a more advanced software course, or better technical training. It's more the question of whether I was truly understanding enough, sensitive enough, intuitive enough, courageous enough, innovative enough, to help this client. It feels more personally devastating as though it's not just a particular skill that was lacking—it was *me*, my very personhood."

You will hear instructors and mentors tell you a lot that it's not your fault when a client takes a nose-dive, or that there was nothing else you could have done, or that there is only so much you can do, or that you aren't perfect and sometimes make mistakes. You will nod your head gratefully. Most of you will agree that this makes sense. But there will be another part of you, a whisper deep inside you, that will wonder whether this all had something to do with you, some inadequacy, some lapse in judgment, some character flaw. Push those thoughts away, if you can; the same sensitivity that becomes your greatest ally in clinical work can also work as a terrible burden.

Hiding in Others' Lives

"I have no life," a nurse admits with a shrug. "The major part of my life is taken up with my work."

Helpers are known to try to save themselves through their work. In Connelly's (1998) novel, *Bringing Out the Dead*, the main character, a medic, tries to save himself by saving others. "I was good at my job," he says. "There were even periods when my hands moved with a speed and skill that were beyond me and my mind worked with a cool authority I had never known."

He feels useful, his life redeemed, for a little while anyway. "I would scrap with depression," he continues, "I drank too much, but every once in a while I participated in a miracle, breathing life back into a young asthmatic, holding a tiny just-born jewel in my hands" (p. 26).

The author, himself an ex-medic, tells the story of despair and hope-lessness that cripples a healer who can't save himself through his acts of service to others. There is the illusion that you can redeem your life, make things all better, through acts of doing good. Yet when the work is done for the day, you face once again those demons that you were trying to escape.

One therapist, who lives alone in a cabin in the mountains, comes down into the valley each day to continue his work with those suffering multiple personality and dissociative disorders. "I've lived alone a long time," he admits, "and yeah, I do get lonely sometimes. Okay, a lot of the time."

He looks thoughtful for a moment, smiles to himself, and then continues with a chuckle. "You know, I'm just more honest about this than most people. Everyone is really alone, even though they delude themselves into thinking they have someone else—a spouse, a roommate, a family—to take the edge off the isolation. I have no such illusions; I know that I'm alone.

"About the only time I feel really connected to the world is when I'm doing therapy. I have these really intense relationships with my clients. I get to know not only their public selves that they show the world, but also their hidden selves that they didn't even admit existed. I'm seeing this one woman, who just showed another personality who only speaks Spanish, even though the host personality claims to not even understand the language ..."

He goes on for a while, amused and fascinated by the details of this complex case, then recalls the question that I asked him. "I like knowing about all this stuff. It's so much more interesting than anything else I do."

"I also like that when the session is over, I'm not responsible anymore. The people go home to their lives. I don't have to deal with them. Until next time."

This therapist finds an outlet for intimacy in his work, yet also makes the sacrifice of any true relationship with a partner. "So I'm alone a lot," he repeats again with a shrug, reassuring himself that his life is indeed fulfilling enough in its present form.

Not Knowing

It is bad enough to know so little, compared to what we would like to understand. It is worse still to feel that tools at our disposal are so limited, so primitive, so inadequate. Just as difficult is the ambiguity of our work, sometimes even the lack of feedback about whether we were helpful or not.

A nurse educator was returning to her office when she heard a cry for help in the stairwell of her building. "I heard a man's voice groaning over and over, 'Help me. Oh God, Oh God, somebody help me.' His voice came from somewhere above me, as if from the sky.

"I stood there frozen, trying to decide whether I should investigate or not. Frankly, I was scared. I teach my nursing students about the importance of self-safety in all helping encounters. I took a deep breath and slowly headed up the stairs, hearing the moans get louder and louder.

"When I got to the next landing, I saw the biggest guy I had ever seen. He must have been six and half feet tall. He was slamming his fists against the wall, crying 'I can't stand it. I just can't stand it anymore.'

"I tried to think of the right therapeutic response. 'Is something wrong?' I asked him, and then groaned to myself. What a stupid thing to say! This guy is climbing the walls and I ask him if something might be wrong.

"I thought about what I might do next when he turned to face me. I am tiny and this man towered over me. We locked eyes for what seemed to me like minutes but it had to be only a few seconds. I will never forget how intense this contact felt. It felt like he was looking inside my heart.

"All of a sudden, he began crying and sobbing again. He slumped down on the stairs and I sat down next to him, a little pixie compared to his gigantic form. I told him we were going to go together to get some help for his pain. He looked at me with this pitiful expression, trusting me immediately. He stood up and followed me down the stairs, crying all the way.

"On the way over to the health center, he told me that he was on a student visa and he had some serious problems with his family back home.

In between disjointed sobs, he also confided that he had just failed an exam. The guy looked completely lost, following me across campus like a puppy—a huge one at that.

"When we arrived at the clinic, I made arrangements for him to get some help. The last I saw of him was when he was led from the reception area into the treatment area. That was the final glimpse I had of the guy and I never heard what happened to him afterwards.

"I often think about this big man. I wonder what happened to him. Did he recover his composure? Did he stay in the country or go home? Is he okay now? I have so many questions and will never know the answers.

"I'm not even sure what this story means to me right now. Except that it reminds me of how often helping remains so ambiguous and unpredictable and mysterious. You just never know."

That's another source of stress and strain in our lives, the not knowing. So many people you will help walk out the door, never to be seen again, leaving you to only imagine what became of them.

Putting Yourself on the Line

Much attention is directed to the risks that clients take in helping relationships: how they must reveal themselves, let down their defenses, share their deepest secrets, confront their worst fears. What about the ways that helpers also allow themselves to be vulnerable?

Therapeutic relationships are collaborative encounters. While it seems as if only the client is the one who takes the risks and opens up, often the helper becomes vulnerable as well. A former therapist in private practice, now retired, talks about the kind of work she has done that often led her to care a little too much. This is especially the case when she made a special effort to extend herself to a client, or a therapist she was supervising, and the gesture went unacknowledged.

"It hurts me when my effort is not appreciated," she says with genuine sorrow. "When someone ignores me, or says 'I don't need your help,' I feel rejected.

"There are times also when I've felt exploited. I'm the one who is giving, giving, giving, and the other person is taking, taking, taking. I feel embarrassed that I extended myself too far. I gave too much.

"When I closed my practice, there was this one other therapist I was supervising and I felt too responsible for her. I kept meeting with her even after I ended things with everyone else. I remained accessible and responsive to her, far more so than was even reasonable. She'd call me when she was stuck. I gave her the best of me. Then, she fell off the face of the earth. She moved somewhere and I haven't heard from her since."

She stops for a moment to regain her composure. It is obvious that even retelling this story after so many years is still bothersome.

"I feel such sadness—right now—I don't know if I feel rejected or ... I don't expect anything in return. But I care so much that it hurts because I made such an investment in her and I misjudged things. I feel doubt about my gesture. I do feel exploited in a way.

"Putting another first is a scary feeling. When I give something of myself and others reject it, I feel ..."

Her voice trails off, as if she feels so much she can't put it all into words. What is clear is that, even with the times in which her efforts were rebuffed, she still has few regrets about giving so much of herself to others.

Self-Doubt

The lack of feedback and follow-up that are sometimes possible also lead to a lot of second-guessing yourself. Did you do the right thing? Did the person not return because you failed him or because he doesn't need any more help? No matter which course of action you choose, there are always another dozen you could have selected instead.

A psychologist doesn't like talking about his self-doubts, most often presenting to the world the image of the supremely confident professional. In a reflective mood, he lets himself say aloud what he often thinks about late at night.

"Two examples from the media will illustrate my perceptions of the sacrifices I make and the price I pay for my work. One, from the rock opera *Jesus Christ Superstar*, is the scene in which everyone within sight is in need of, asking for, demanding help. The other, from the play *Equus*, is the scene at the end in which the psychiatrist struggles with the question about whether one person truly has the right to be in control of the behavior of another. For those who accept the role as a helper of others, the demands on time and energy can become nearly overwhelming. Success in this role can put in jeopardy the capability to respond to the needs of self and family. The extent to which this occurs is, at least to some degree, under the control of the helper. The other concern, though, is more difficult. Our guidance often does lead persons toward a particular path. Lives are changed, and the change may be painful. Was the change appropriate? Was the outcome of change worth the pain it elicited? In the stillness of the night, this self-questioning and self-doubt can exact a heavy toll on me."

I'm sure you know exactly what he is talking about. Already, you have second-guessed yourself a thousand times. Any time you offer help to someone, you wonder if you handled it "correctly," meaning that you responded most effectively. Did you read the situation correctly? Was there something you missed? Could you have phrased things differently? Did you even make the best choice of intervention?

When you consult with supervisors or colleagues about your case, you often feel worse once you realize all the other things you never even considered. As you play back the interaction you can always think of so many other ways that you could have responded with greater sensitivity and skill. The hardest part is letting all of this go and moving on, accepting the limits of what you can do, acknowledging your limitations.

☐ Protecting Yourself Against Discouragement and Burnout

Whereas the condition characterized by disillusionment, despair, cynicism, powerlessness, and emotional and physical depletion, is usually called "burn-out" (Maslach, 1982), it is actually a state that develops slowly rather than in one instantaneous flare-up. "Burnout is not something that happens to you all of a sudden; rather, it results from an insidious form of self-neglect, a kind of a slow deterioration that eventually rusts and corrodes the edges of your compassion and caring" (Kottler & Zehm, 2000, p. 82).

Every beginner vows this will never happen to him or her. After all, you are different. You aren't like all these washed-out, negative zombies who just go through the motions of doing their jobs, emptying the psychic bedpans of people without a single ounce of compassion. You will never be like that.

Don't you think that once upon a time *everyone* felt like you do now? After all, who would launch a career as a helper if they weren't excited about the idea of doing good and wanting to save the world? Everyone starts out with enthusiasm and determination that they will maintain their momentum and retain the joy for serving others, not just right now but forever. So what happens along the way of this journey that leads some people astray?

After 10 years in full-time private practice, I can't point to any particular time when it hit me that I had burned out, or rather "rusted out." At some interval along the way, I stopped caring very much about some of the people I was helping. I found it hard to listen to them, even harder to feel compassion for those who complained or whined. I fantasized a lot during sessions, trying to escape interactions that I found tedious and boring. When people canceled appointments, I felt like celebrating.

When I got together with colleagues, I was dismayed to find that my experience was not that unusual. We would sit around and spend more time talking about how to drum up business than how to help people currently in our charge. We'd talk about our clients in critical ways, sometimes even ridicule them or call them names.

I know this is something you should not be hearing at this optimistic stage of your training, just starting out with stars in your eyes for all the magic you will do to heal the wounds of the suffering. What I didn't realize is that, in the words of Ram Das and Gorman (1985), "The experience of burnout has a particular kind of poignancy. Having started out to help others, we're somehow getting wounded ourselves" (pp. 185–186).

How does this rustout happen, you must wonder with a degree of trepidation? How can you make yourself immune to the toxic effects of this work, which strike deep into the hearts of the most committed and noble helpers?

What got me in the most trouble was the belief that I was invulnerable. I was different from everyone else. I cared more than anyone. Naturally, the more you care, the more deeply you feel others' pain, the more at-risk you place yourself as a potential victim for "compassion fatigue."

How can you stand underneath the inexorable drip of other people's anguish, despair, and hopelessness without beginning to show wear and rust in the process? That's why many helpers wear protection. They so insulate themselves from the people they help, so distance themselves, that the firm boundaries protect them from psychic pollution.

Obviously, you want to try to find some sort of balance between a helping stance of compassionate engagement with an appropriate degree of detachment. After all, their problems are not yours; you have your own stuff to deal with. This is much harder to do than you can possibly imagine.

I wish I had noticed the first signs of rustout as I began to show symptoms. Remember, this process begins slowly, with little signs of deterioration along your edges. You notice yourself feeling impatient with those you help. You can hear yourself become critical and judgmental inside your head. When you listen to yourself talk about clients, you can occasionally hear a tone of disdain. You start "checking out" more and more. Under the guise of being "realistic," you have given up your grand plans to change the world.

One of the easiest ways to get yourself in trouble in the first place is to have expectations and goals that you, or most anyone, could never reach. That is a set-up for disappointment and failure. On the other hand, it is dreaming big that makes it possible for the most dramatic helping efforts to take place.

If you sense mixed messages from me—dream big, but rein in your expectations—you are hearing this accurately. I don't have easy answers for preventing rustout and compassion fatigue; neither does anyone else. The best we can offer is to follow several guidelines (Corey & Corey, 1998;

Kottler, 1993, 1999; Maslach, 1982). Although further advice is offered in the last chapter, here are a few things to keep in mind:

Honestly Assess Your Own Symptoms.   Some key signs to watch for include:

- feelings of isolation and alienation;
- escapist fantasies;
- repeated blaming, complaining, and whining;
- low energy and passion;
- impatience towards clients and colleagues;
- cynicism and discouragement;
- sleep disruption or other signs of stress.

Examine Your Fears of Failure.   All helpers must deal with feelings of ineptitude, incompetence, self-doubt, and discouragement. Although the work climate is often not a safe one in which to talk about your imperfections and mistakes, you must find folks in whom you can confide. In this type of work, setbacks, disappointments, and failures are inevitable; if you don't think so, you are lying to yourself. They key is to learn from these experiences.

Be Realistic About What You Can and Cannot Do.   Probably one of my greatest weaknesses as a helper is not knowing my own limits. I delude myself into thinking I can save the world, or at least rescue a lost soul from the depths of despair. I believe I have the power to heal suffering. When someone does not improve quickly enough, I also imagine that it is because I'm not trying hard enough. It's all my responsibility when things go right, and all my fault when things go wrong. This, of course, is pretty delusional thinking, not to mention incredibly narcissistic.

The truth is that most of the work is done by the client. Or at least that is what I teach to others. It is the hardest thing to let go, to accept that you or I have done what we can, what anyone could have done, and then allow the other person in pain to do the rest. Or not to do the rest, if that is the choice.

Confront Your Own Personal Reactions to Those You Help.   Whether it is called *countertransference*, or more simply a strong feeling towards what you are doing or who you are doing it with, you must acknowledge what you are experiencing and take steps to counteract reactions that might be getting in the way.

It is often helpful to consider what the situation reminds you of, or who the person resembles from the past, in order to discover unresolved issues.

When You're Feeling Stuck, Work Things Through With a Partner or Supervisor.   Don't sit around whining and complaining. Instead, solicit the sort of help that forces you to consider what you are doing that is counterproductive and what you might try instead to break through impasses.

Change What You're Doing or the Way You're Doing It.   Boredom slips in when you rely too much on routines and predictable patterns. Be creative. Try different strategies. Take some risks. Have some fun.

Diversify Your Life.   Just as underinvestment in doing good can mean a lack of commitment, an overinvestment can signal trouble. Make sure that you have structured your life in such a way that helping others plays an important role but does not become the *only* thing you have.

Build a Support System.   Take care of yourself in the same ways that you advocate to others. While confiding in colleagues feels good because they understand just what you are going through, make sure you also hang out with "civilians" who help to diversify your life. Otherwise, you end up breathing, eating, and talking about your work all the time and not taking needed breaks.

Reduce the Stress That You Face.   You have seen how stress in a helper's life originates from several main sources: (a) personal transitions and problems, (b) the work environment, (c) the people you help, (d) the people you work with, and (e) your own expectations. Surprisingly, the easiest place to begin your efforts at reducing stress is to start with your own beliefs that lead to perceptions of failure. When you hold unrealistic expectations for what you can do ("I can save people from their misery"; "I can cure people from their suffering"), you are setting yourself up for a lot of grief.

When you look at another source of stress, say the frustrations and despair you feel in relation to those you help who are not improving, the first place to start is to again examine your own expectations for them. Quite often, you will find that you are demanding things of them that they are unable or unwilling to do. In other words, rather than meeting them at a place where they are eager and motivated to work, you insist that they join you somewhere that *you* feel most comfortable. They may be trying to cooperate, but just not in a way that you prefer. Then you call it "resistance" or label them as "obstructive" or "difficult."

This is not to say that a great amount of the stress you face is not the result of circumstances in how and where you work. If your colleagues are not supportive, if your supervisor is incompetent or ornery, if your workload is overwhelming, then some degree of dissatisfaction is likely to be present no matter how you try to frame things.

Just as you would with someone you are helping, your job is to figure out what is within your power to change in order to reduce stress levels in your life and work. Once you have identified these targets, then develop a plan to make significant alterations or minor adjustments. One practitioner, for example, looked at the ways he was operating and decided that he would take the following steps in each area:

1. Personal transitions and problems

   - Reduce my living expenses so I feel less money pressure.
   - Stabilize sleep patterns.
   - Reduce alcohol consumption.
   - Spend more time with friends and less time with parents.

2. Work environment

   - Stop taking on new projects until I've finished ones I've started.
   - Build more variation into my activities so I feel more stimulated.
   - Stop doing paperwork at home on the weekends.

3. Clients

   - Set clearer limits and boundaries.
   - Use more variety of interventions.
   - Go to workshops to learn some newer methods.
   - Let go of those I can't help.

4. Colleagues

   - Confront my supervisor about overloading me.
   - Get away from the staff lounge where people complain so much.
   - Invite some people I don't know well out to lunch.

5. Expectations

   - Remind myself that I am doing all I can.
   - Remember that it's not my job to change people.
   - Accept my limits and imperfections.

If the System Is Dysfunctional, Go Somewhere Else to Do Good.
Sometimes it is unreasonable, or even impossible, to initiate the sort of changes you would need in order to work in more healthy ways. The work setting may be so toxic that minor adjustments will not make a significant difference. Perhaps the administrative staff is truly heartless, the resources are so inadequate, or the mission of the organization dooms it to failure. In other words, you've got to get the heck out of there.

In such circumstances it is wise to stop complaining, stop whining, stop blaming others. There is nothing more unattractive, and more senseless, then sitting around in a place that is not good for you and telling anyone who will listen how unhappy you are. They may sympathize, even trade complaints with you, but nothing much will change unless you take constructive steps to better meet your own needs.

CHAPTER 7

Excuses and Obstacles to Overcome

Almost everyone would agree that doing good is a wonderful thing. For all of the reasons highlighted previously, helping people is what makes the world go 'round. Our community and environment cannot be sustained without cooperative action in which we all pitch in to help one another out. Besides, it feels good to make a difference in other people's lives.

The previous chapter highlighted some of the sacrifices that helpers make as a result of their commitment to service. These are no secret, which is one reason why some people are reluctant to get involved in the first place, or why people who do good don't do even more. In this chapter we examine some of the obstacles and excuses that prevent you and others from making even more significant differences in the world.

☐ First the Obstacles, Then the Excuses

Numerous studies have been undertaken to examine why many gentiles, estimated to number in the several hundred thousand, risked their lives and those of their families to rescue or harbor Jews during the Holocaust (S. P. Oliner & Oliner, 1988). Of equal interest to Rosenman (1999) were the obstacles that prevented more people from becoming involved in altruistic behavior.

Of course the first obstacle to saving lives was that if you were caught doing so, you and your whole family would likely face interrogation, torture, and then execution. If you were lucky, you would be shipped off to the same concentration camps that awaited those you were trying to save. So certainly self-preservation acts as a powerful deterrent to becoming involved in any activity in which you put yourself and loved ones at risk.

A second factor that reveals much more about the dark side of human beings is that we seem to have an incredible fascination with watching violence, as long as we remain at a safe distance. Just as today violent movies, true crime books, even crime scenes, attract huge audiences that want a glimpse of a dead body, many people have a perverse attraction toward watching others' misfortune. If you doubt this then consider how often traffic slows down at the scene of accidents so that onlookers can observe the mayhem.

Among the Holocaust rescuers and others who engage in altruistic acts, it is important to feel appreciation from the victims even if there is no larger recognition. Since Jews were not in a position to even find their rescuers again, much less thank them for their efforts, that acted as an obstacle for more people getting involved. Surely, part of the pleasure in giving, whether that is a gift or an act of kindness, is in seeing the expression of appreciation on the other person's face. In the case of saving Jews, not only were there no reciprocal benefits possible, but there was often no explicit gratitude.

Another obstacle was the dehumanization of the victims. If biases, prejudices, and racism act to diminish the value of some human lives, then less effort will be expended to help them. Because there was such an emphasis placed on differences between Jews and others, there was less sympathy and empathy felt towards their plight. If you feel more grief and distress about the oppression faced by one group in Bosnia, the Middle East, or East Chicago over others, it is often because you identify more closely with these people.

There is a code of behavior for victims, some of which elicits sympathy and instinctive help, while other actions stir up disdain, anger, and repulsion. Compare, for example, your instinctual responses to a child who falls in the water and is apparently drowning, versus a young boy who is crying and whimpering because he is being teased. In Nazi Germany, the Aryan code of respecting one kind of strength let citizens view Jewish pacifism and compliance as a sign that they deserved what they got.

One other barrier is the way helpful behavior is cast by the larger culture. In Germany, helping Jews was viewed as a criminal, if not psychotic, act. In our own culture, we may question the sanity of people who jeopardize their safety in order to help someone they never even met. Kohn (1990) has made the point that when you think that you are special you are considered to have a healthy self-concept, when you believe your country is superior you are labeled a patriot, but when you think well of humankind, you are dismissed as hopelessly naive.

When we look beyond our own culture, we find that standards of what is considered altruistic vary considerably. In much of Asia, for example, help is limited to members of one's own "tribe." In fact, it is inconceivable to many why we would ever want to help others who are not part of our race, religion, or creed. In writing about the ways that China and Russia reacted to United States' involvement in the Kosovo War, former Secretary of State Henry Kissinger (1999) writes about the causes for Chinese and Russian misunderstanding of U.S. motives: "Their leaders are products of societies that interpret decisions about war and peace according to whether they enhance a nation's security or other vital interests. If they can discern no such traditional rationale to U.S. behavior, they ascribe our motives not to altruism but to a hidden agenda for domination."

Perhaps the Chinese leaders are correct in their cynical assessment that all intervention takes place out of national self-interest. Nevertheless, there are certainly cultural differences that get in the way of global efforts to offer aid to the disadvantaged.

Sarason (1995) mentions one other force that plays a role: the institutional and cultural policies that discourage helping professionals from demonstrating greater caring and compassion in their work. Among them are the following:

1. reduced funds for mental health and education;
2. managed care organizations that have valued efficiency over quality of services;
3. bean-counting management by MBAs in charge of community services;
4. competition for resources and cut-throat marketing among helpers;
5. political squabbles that dehumanize the workplace;
6. scientific traditions that make measurement, objectivity, and empiricism more important than subjective factors;
7. the litigious atmosphere in which you can't fully trust the people you help. They will sue you if they don't like the way they believe they have been treated, regardless of your noble intent and best efforts.

☐ The Excuses

The obstacles previously mentioned largely result from constraints placed by others. However, these are not the only reasons why people are reluctant to be more helpful to others; there are also internal excuses and defenses operating that prevent constructive action.

Someone Else Will Do It

The "bystander effect" was so named to describe the ways that the inclination to offer help is influenced by the behavior of others in the vicinity. In their classic study of why people do not offer assistance, even when someone is dying before their very eyes, Latané and Darley (1970) tried to make sense of the excuse that spectators offer when they say, "It's none of my business."

What prompted this research was a case in New York in which a young woman, Kitty Genovese, was stabbed to death in front of 38 witnesses who watched the murder unfold. Although she screamed over and over again, "I'm dying," "I'm dying," and "Please help me," "Somebody please help me!" nobody came to her rescue. In fact, nobody even bothered to call the police until after she had been dying in a pool of her own blood for a half hour! Needless to say, when this story hit the news it created quite a ruckus.

The bystanders were accused of being irresponsible and callous, to say the least. Yet this behavior is not unusual in human history, as the Holocaust and other acts of genocide will attest. Over and over again, people offer excuses that it's none of their business, or someone else will do something; it's not their responsibility.

Yet, as Latané and Darley (1970) discovered, it was the very presence of so many people that made it possible to avoid responsibility for intervening. It wasn't apathy, alienation, or uncaring people at work in their collective passivity; rather it was the dehumanization of the victim and the impersonality of contemporary life.

I recall a time walking through the Student Union Building on campus at the height of daily activity. There were hundreds of students bustling back and forth, hurrying on their way to class, study groups, or to grab some food. As I took a shortcut through the building to escape the desert heat, I noticed a young woman sitting in a chair hunched over. She was crying, sobbing actually, obviously distressed. As I passed her by, it took a minute to register that she was upset. Even more disturbing to me is that literally hundreds of people were watching this scene every minute but nobody was doing anything—including me!

I made an about-face, approached the woman, and asked what I could do to help. As it turns out, she didn't seem to want any assistance, although I sat with her for a few minutes just so she wouldn't be alone. Now, contrast this scene with one in which you are the *only* one in the building at the time you see a distressed person. Clearly, you would be more inclined to offer help when there are not others around. And this is exactly what has been supported by hundreds of studies on the bystander effect (Hunt, 1990; Latané, 1981).

I Didn't Know There Was a Problem

Whether during the Holocaust, a case of child abuse in your own neighborhood, or any other situation, it is easy to bury our heads in the sand, to tell ourselves that what is happening is none of our business. Interestingly, until the invention of the door, domestic abuse was impossible to hide. We all lived in caves, or out in the open, where everyone in the community was able to monitor behavior. It would have been inconceivable that anyone could have abused another without the rest of the world looking on. Once doors were invented, privacy became not only a matter of personal rights, but also of clandestine activity.

The function of our media, not to mention informal gossip, is to keep us informed about what is going on around us. This intelligence has historically been crucial for members of our species to protect themselves against marauding bands, impending disaster, stormy weather, or even people around us plotting revenge. Those who were not exquisitely sensitive to others and aware of their surroundings were likely to be the first ones picked off by predators or inclement weather.

We now have the luxury of selectively tuning in to only those stimuli that interest us, ignoring the rest. If we prefer not to see poverty, we can stay out of that part of the city. If we would rather not hear about injustices, we can skip that part of the paper. If we don't like to hear bad news, we can change the channel and choose our companions carefully. This is, of course, your right. Nevertheless, people continue to suffer largely through our benign neglect. If we truly opened our eyes and ears and hearts to what is going on around us, we would have little choice but to act. We would also be exhausted, but that leads to the next point.

I Don't Have Time

Those helpers most prone to burnout are those who overschedule their lives, who give away so much of their time and energy that they have nothing leftover for themselves. They experience compassion fatigue, meaning that they become so emotionally, physically, and spiritually depleted that they become empty shells.

"I'd like to do more to help people," one retired policeman confides who now volunteers his time to help needy kids, "but there's only so much I can give. You won't believe the shit I've seen in my life. It would make you sick."

He trails off at the end of the sentence, lost in the flashbacks of brutal violence and inhumanity he has witnessed. No matter how hard I press him, he is unwilling to go into this further. "Let's just say that I'd like to do more, but right now I just don't have the time."

That, of course, is a code for "I don't want to," which is hardly so much an excuse as a legitimate reason for limiting involvement that goes beyond the point where we can handle the effects. After all, you are no good to anyone else if you don't take care of yourself first. One of the temptations for beginners is to take on too many responsibilities and to avoid saying no when it is clearly appropriate to do so.

Obviously, a balance must be reached between what you can reasonably do for others without depleting your own resources to the point where you can't easily recover, and the responsibility to make time for those people who most need your help.

I Don't Know Enough

"I'm only a student," you might say to yourself, or "I don't have enough to offer." While this much is true—you will *never* have enough to offer—sometimes what people need most is basic human contact. A smile can work wonders. We are talking about reaching out to others to let them know they are not alone.

You have seen that the process of helping often involves not so much solving others' problems or fixing their difficulties as empowering them to do the work. You can (and should) spend a lifetime refining the helping skills needed to facilitate this process, but at the most basic level, listening works wonders, especially when you can prove to others that they have been understood.

The reality is that you will never know enough to do the kind of job that you want to do. You will never master helping skills to the degree that you would like. You will constantly be aware of your lapses, miscalculations, misjudgments, and failings. All the books you read, courses you take, workshops you attend, degrees and licenses you collect, supervision and personal counseling you experience, will still not prepare you to the point where you feel as ready as you would like to be of service.

Personally, I am appalled when I think back on my early cases and consider the primitive things I tried. There isn't a session that still goes by that I can't point out several mistakes I made and identify a half dozen alternative paths I wish I had taken. Does that mean that I have failed my clients? Absolutely not. One of the things we try to teach others is that we do the best we can, with what we know and understand at the time; if we could have done anything else, we would have. Such forgiveness teaches us to learn from our mistakes.

Naturally, you would want to be careful when you are helping others. Don't exceed your training and limitations. Don't push anyone to do something for which they are not ready. Don't impose your values on others; respect their priorities. Remain sensitive to the impact of your efforts. Watch and listen carefully to how others are responding to your helpful attempts. Don't be afraid to ask how things are going.

It isn't an excuse that you don't know enough. That is your own humility reminding you to be careful.

People Deserve What They Get

Other variations of this theme include: "They must have done something to provoke this misfortune." "The gods must be angry." "It must be fate." This is the favorite excuse of bystanders who somehow must rationalize what is going on, much less their own inaction.

This is not a common ploy among helpers, professionals or volunteers, since we already exhibit a high degree of compassion and empathy for others. Nevertheless, there are subtle ways that we rationalize avoiding more committed service. You will hear this a lot among some veterans who have probably stayed too long in their jobs. They have become cynical, although they will label you as naive. "You'll find out how bad some of these people are," they'll warn you. "These folks will eat you alive if you half let 'em. You watch yourself now."

Helpers are members of the middle class, sometimes the very upper echelons of the economic class. Whereas once upon a time, teachers, priests, and monks swore vows of poverty in order to do their good deeds, helpers are now routinely driving around in hot sports cars or utility vehicles, living in the nicest suburban areas, making a decent living.

Many of us have this ambivalent relationship with the material world. We have devoted our lives to service rather than attaining wealth, yet we still covet the finer things in life, as well as experience envy, jealousy, and resentment for the things we can't afford. Still, we represent a degree of success. We are admired for our devotion and commitment. We are seen as wise and noble. We are healers and gurus from whom others seek enlightenment. This is not the result of pure luck (many of us have the good fortune to be living in prosperous countries), but a consequence of our hard work. We have managed to overcome adversity, so why can't others?

It is a dark side of the helping professions, not often admitted much less ever discussed aloud, that we might feel disdain for the weak and helpless. It is hard not to feel impatient with the often slow progress that we witness.

"You've been in this loveless, abusive marriage for how many years?" you ask incredulously.

"We've been over this same point 11 times," you remind the person with confidence since you have kept meticulous score.

"You say you want things to be different," you say with more than a hint of frustration, "but you refuse to do anything to make that happen."

Some veteran helpers reach the point where they see their clients as spineless. "They just need a good kick in the ass," you will hear. "Don't coddle them; they'll just take advantage of you, get you to do their work for them."

I am not implying that it is our job to be responsible for others' progress, nor that we should be the ones doing their work. Rather, I am describing the kind of cynicism that can easily infect your spirit as your work evolves over time, especially when people don't change as quickly as you would like. You will know that you are well on your way to rustout when you start thinking to yourself, maybe even muttering aloud when you think nobody is listening, "These people deserve what they get."

It Won't Matter Anyway

Ah, the essential existential dilemma. For most of us, there is serious and ongoing speculation about the good we are doing for others. In the absence of sufficient and accurate feedback on the impact of our interventions, we are left to wonder about the difference we make in others' lives. During times of doubt, it may very well seem as if your efforts are futile. What difference does it really make if you help one person, given all the need that exists in the world?

People routinely excuse themselves from becoming more involved in acts of service because they don't feel their tiny commitment will matter much in the grand scope of things. This is the sort of thing you have heard in sermons before, stuff about doing your share to make the world a better place, taking one small step to show others, and so on. Just about the time that the spirit of Jesus, Moses, Ghandi, or Florence Nightingale is invoked, I tend to drift off. I'm tired of being lectured to, told that I'm not doing my fair share. I always wonder to what extent the politicians and clergy who tell us to do more are practicing in their lives what they preach to us. Why are we sitting in this comfortable, luxurious room talking about how noble this stuff is instead of getting out into the world to actually do something constructive?

However inevitable and unavoidable, you will drive yourself crazy if you continue to dwell on how insignificant your helping efforts are in light of how much more needs to be done. If you can offer comfort to one life, if you can alleviate a little suffering in one family, if you can rescue one person from the depths of despair, heck, if you can pick up one cigarette butt lying in the street, you have done a small part to make the world a better place. This might not sound like a big deal, but remember, you are doing this as much for yourself as for others. I don't know about you, but it feels very good to me when once a day, or even several times per day, I can do *something* useful.

What's In It for Me?

We have seen how there are selfish and self-centered reasons why people do good that have little to do with altruism. In the process of helping others, we are helping ourselves. There is little shame in this; it is the reality of the way we are built that we tend to look out for our own interests.

Yet, if you measure every act in terms of what's in it for you, you would lead a very narcissistic existence. The most gracious gestures, whether opening a door for a stranger or jumping into a lake to save someone's life, are done thoughtlessly, without regard for personal benefit. It just seems like the right thing to do at the time.

Doing good, in the best sense of what that means, is really *not* about you at all. It represents one of those rare times when you don't even exist, when you forget about your own troubles and needs and desires. For a brief moment or two, you put your self aside, instead choosing (and it is a clear choice) to put someone else first. You do this sort of thing all the time for friends and family (remember kinship bonds and reciprocal altruism from Chapter 2?). The truly miraculous act of selfless giving is when you extend yourself to a perfect stranger without regard for what is in it for you.

☐ Confronting Excuses

Being the bright, creative person you are, if you are going to come up with reasons for avoiding doing something you would rather not do, they are going to be very good ones. Of course, while a certain degree of ambivalence is quite normal, if your resistance to helping is of sufficient magnitude, it is probably a good idea to try another field in which selfishness is rewarded— and there are plenty of those.

There is nothing intrinsically noble about calling yourself helper, unless the work you do is for other than personal gain. There are plenty of professionals who have gotten very wealthy and powerful by exploiting others along the way; the work they do has little to do with helping anyone and everything to do with feeding their own egos and bank accounts. I am certain you know individuals who fit this profile: they may call themselves "counselors," "therapists," "teachers," "philanthropists," or other helpers, but they are really only looking out for their own interests. If anyone is helped along the way, that's fine, but not the real point.

Of course, there isn't exactly a dichotomy between helping yourself and helping others. You are allowed to be paid a reasonable wage for your time and energy, whether that compensation is in the form of a salary, social approval, or a way to structure your time. There are helpers who earn a very good living but who still keep their perspective clear about what they are doing that matters most. Similarly, there are volunteers working without any compensation whatsoever, even paying some of their own expenses, who are still doing their work for very self-centered reasons that have little to do with altruism. Someone could be working in a soup kitchen with the homeless, for instance, not because he cares about the people he is serving, but because he has a crush on one of the other workers he hopes to impress.

Where I am leading with this is that it is crucial that you give considerable thought to your own motives for choosing to be a helper. This includes looking at not only the noble reasons that you tell others for your devotion, but also the very personal benefits you enjoy. When you are truly honest with yourself, you are in the best position possible to confront some of the excuses you offer for why you don't do so much more.

An Internal Debate

It is not easy to decide to make personal sacrifices on behalf of others. There is always a price paid, if not in immediate ways, then in long-term effects. A counselor and educator decided to give up her comfortable position in order to devote her time to working in a Third World country with more needy groups. This would involve relocating her family, as well as putting herself into debt. Yet she felt little doubt about the decision they all made together. Actually, she was more puzzled by the way that others reacted to her choice, as if what she was doing might be threatening to them.

"Sometimes I wonder if the notion of personal sacrifices and the price paid for helping are artifacts of the outsider," she mused. "It's just an excuse to not take action."

I thought about this for a moment and wondered if this was really true. Indeed, what looks like sacrifice to some people might actually be a privilege for another.

With complete conviction, she reports, "I make decisions to structure my life in ways that are dictated by my passion and the meaning that comes from the work I choose. My work is helping others. Outsiders may believe that taking time away from my career to move with my family to Latin America for volunteer work is a high price to pay. Will my children be safe? What will this do to their education? Won't this hurt my career deviating from the route to promotion? And won't this kill us financially, taking a leave without pay when we have so many loans and a mortgage?

"What I know is that my children and I will learn important lessons about life when we are away from the comfort of our upper middle class existence, that there are many paths in my career—tenure is only one—and that money can't buy the experience that our volunteer work in Latin America will bring. For me, avoiding risk and resisting passion have a price that is too high for me and my family to pay."

During your own internal debate about the risks you are willing to take and the sacrifices you are willing to make on behalf of your commitment to doing good, there are several questions you might wish to consider. Each is linked to the excuses that were mentioned earlier.

• What are your main priorities in life?
• What would you want others to do for you?
• How do you believe that big changes occur?
• What would the world be like if everyone minded their own business?
• What do you find so threatening about others' pain?
• What do you need to know in order for it to be enough?
• What would it take for you to feel like helping more?

Think deeply about the answers to these questions. Talk to friends and loved ones about your conclusions. Ask them what they think as well.

Take What You Can Get

I was talking to a teacher who is committed to spending as much of his time talking to kids informally as he can. He knows that the most good he does is not part of his lesson plans, but rather during his conversations before and after class in which he hears about the kids' lives. So much of the time, however, he feels like his efforts are futile. The kids go home to rotten homes. If they have any adults present in their lives, they often sabotage whatever good is attempted. Nevertheless, this teacher keeps trying to make contact with the most troubled children who most need his help.

The teacher remembered a story I once told about how in my work I often feel so frustrated because I can't really tell who I have helped and who I have not. Especially when dealing with people who have emotional problems, it sometimes takes a long time to know what sort of difference has been made. Besides, you rarely hear feedback from people afterwards.

I had been musing about how much I enjoy giving directions to people who are lost. I'm really good at it. I address their fears with all my clinical skills. I give precise instructions, complete with landmarks and even things to see along the way. Most of all, I like the part in which I know I have helped someone. I *know* that as a result of my helping efforts, they will get to where they are going. But that is so rarely the case (or at least much less often than I'd prefer) with the normal helping I do as a teacher or writer or therapist.

"I remember what you said about giving someone directions," the teacher reminded me. "At least you definitely knew you helped someone. I can really relate to that."

I commiserate with him that the futility and lack of feedback can indeed be so frustrating. He readily agreed.

"I was talking to this one student after class yesterday," he continued, "and she told me about her journey with anorexia/bulimia. I just listened and gave her some encouragement, and though this was not a formal counseling session I felt that I had helped, done some good. She walked away with a smile on her face and so did I."

In this case, a teacher finds a way to confront the obstacles that block his passion and commitment to do good for others. He knows that most of the time he will never know what impact he has had on students, but he takes what he can get. Gratefully. What about you?

Where Can You Go Next?

This is the practical chapter in the book, the one that violates the rule about not giving advice to those you are helping because they rarely listen anyway and it only reinforces the idea that they don't know what is best for themselves. I happen to believe very strongly that most people do know what is best for themselves, especially if they are given the opportunity to reflect thoughtfully within the context of a helping relationship (such as the one between author and reader).

It is helpful to know what works for others in a position similar to your own. For instance, in surveys of psychologists (Pearlman, 1995) and trauma therapists (Williams & Sommer, 1995) it was found that several activities were most effective in dealing with the stresses and strains of their jobs. Not surprisingly, the following were listed most frequently:

- Take regular vacations.
- Engage in social activities.
- Get supervision from someone who understands.
- Diversify interests to include non-work-related activities.
- Change work schedule.
- Get more involved in spiritual pursuits.
- Follow a physical exercise program every day.
- Write in a journal.
- Find creative outlets.
- Get in therapy.

The advice offered by experienced professional and volunteer helpers is not intended to be followed as a blueprint. Rather, it is the best attempt of those who have devoted their lives to doing good to reflect on what they wish they had known earlier and what they would have liked to have done a little differently. Essentially, I asked several dozen helpers to think about what single thing they would most like to pass on to others who are just beginning their careers. This is what a few of them had to say for themselves.

Take What You Do Seriously

"Take your work very seriously," advises a veteran therapist. "People are, in effect, putting their lives in your hands. Learn from your experience. Carefully analyze the outcomes of each case with a goal of being more effective with the next one. Focus on the things which you already do well and hone your skills so you do them even better. And, while I believe you must take your work seriously, avoid the trap of taking yourself too seriously. Life will go on, good and sometimes bad things will happen, regardless of what you do."

☐ Keep Your Sense of Humor

This may sound like a contradiction of the previous advice that tells you to take what you do seriously. You can treat your helping work reverently, honor your clients, and still retain the ability to laugh at the absurdities of what transpires. In fact, one definition of emotional disturbance is that people take themselves too seriously.

Just think about how absurd the whole enterprise of helping really is.

1. We don't really understand how helping works, and why it doesn't. The best that we have are some theories, many of which directly contradict one another.
2. Helpers work in such different ways, employing so many different inter-ventions, yet they all seem effective some of the time with some people. You can confront someone, reflect feelings, interpret hidden messages, reframe problems, or delve into the unconscious. You can work in the present, past, or future. You can work with families, couples, groups, or individuals. You can use a variety of methods, employ a menagerie of techniques, adopt a dozen different styles—and they all have their disci-ples and true believers, as well as satisfied customers. If that isn't absurd and humorous, I don't know what else is.
3. We never really know if we help someone or not. The ones we think were helped the most may be faking or kidding themselves; the ones we think we failed may turn out to have ultimately changed the most.

The whole idea of helping someone by merely listening and responding seems humorous. Play and fun are an integral part of helping; it need not be grim. A community volunteer advises beginners to make sure that you're having fun and enjoying what you're doing. "If you're not, then you can become resentful of those you are helping. Your empathy can become compromised. You lose the ability to put a twinkle in their eye and a smile on their face."

Do What's Unnatural

"Helping skills can be taught," says an educator who specializes in techniques classes. "Some people are natural helpers. When natural helpers learn helping skills, we have a potent combination! However, that developmental process can be scary. Natural helpers have accumulated years of practicing things that work but aren't necessarily the most effective strategies. Letting go of those well-practiced, natural, and reinforced tendencies while learning more effective skills—I'm thinking about basic listening skills as opposed to questioning and advice giving—without the advantage of polished new skills creates a temporary void. Learning to be a professional helper is a developmental process. Practice and learn; when the learned skills and natural abilities come together, magic occurs for both the one who is helped and the helper."

In learning to help, there are habits you must let go of in addition to new skills to acquire. You learn to be more patient. You learn to listen rather than talk so much. Finally, you master the intricacies of helping people figure out things for themselves.

Don't Expect Too Much

If you are honest you will admit that one reason why you like to help is because it feels good to see the smile of appreciation on someone's face. Even if it's a barely acknowledged nod, you feel fulfilled for a moment. If you deny this, think about what it's like when you graciously let someone cut in front of you, whether in line or traffic, and they don't even give you a glance. Recall those times when you have extended yourself in a big way, invested a lot of time and energy on someone's behalf, and they don't give you the slightest word of thanks. Even if you don't need such gratitude, it still tastes like icing on the cake.

Once you admit that you do good deeds because you enjoy making people happy—no shame in that—you can begin to monitor what it is you honestly expect as a result of your efforts. The more you can moderate those expectations, the more you will draw your sustained energy from internal rather than external sources.

An experienced teacher talks about how she has learned over time to temper her expectations as much as possible:

"Sometimes I've lost friends who were disappointed when I didn't continually give and they seemed to resent that I also gave to others, not them alone. I learned long ago not to expect anything back . . . and it was a great freedom when I grasped this simple yet liberating attitude. And what I find is that all sorts of things *do* come back but in the most unexpected, creative, spontaneous, and remarkable ways, and not always from the people you'd expect.

"A very small example is a student I had last year who was very shy—she blushed bright red whenever I spoke to her and so I didn't speak with her very often as I seemed to make her nervous. She hardly said a thing to me. I did spend a little time with her going over her journal assignment at her request, but nothing more than I've done with hundreds of students. I felt that I hardly knew her. At the end of the year she presented me with this angel candle stick and gold candle and a gorgeous card with all these words about what a difference I'd made in her life. Well, I felt like quite the fraud, yet I had to acknowledge that this was the student's perception, not mine. I guess we touch people in the most unexpected ways and even when we're not looking.

"Jon Kabat Zinn said something like, 'There is no giving and receiving—it's just the universe rearranging itself.' I feel that's a liberating statement as it frees one to both help and be helped without feeling self-righteous or indebted or expected to be grateful. The times I have expected people to be grateful (and they weren't) really stung. In fact, it quite depressed me. I felt used and abused. But then I realized that if I only did for others in the hope of their gratitude then I shouldn't help them at all. Expect nothing and it sets you free."

Expect a Lot but Get Used to Disappointment

I have mentioned before that high expectations may lead to disappointment but they also set the highest standards possible. One experienced volunteer talks about how he handles this dilemma:

"It's not always easy to help and you do not always have success or even know that you have had succeeded. The main thing to ask yourself is, 'Am I doing this for me or them?' The answer to this question determines how long you will survive. In the end doing good is not always rewarding, as you tend to get more feedback when you do it wrong."

Find and Sustain Your Passion

The heart of what we do is about passion and commitment. So many helpers mention these factors again and again.

"If passion comes to you from helping others," says one representative voice, "find a way to make it happen again and again. Don't look for outcomes as rewards for your work with others: Allow yourself to be filled with the joy and passion that will naturally come to you when you help others—that joy will inspire you to do more! Aim small and give yourself permission to change course, stop, or try something new. Finally, remember that helping others means helping others find their own way, not find *your* way."

Know How Much You Can Take

One of the voices you heard earlier in the book of an overstressed and overscheduled helper admonishes beginners to avoid the mistakes that he has made.

"Don't expect that doing good means that you and others around you will not be hurt. Doing good often puts you in the most difficult situations rather than putting you in the ones which are more comfortable for you. You will be hurt in many ways and you will have to decide and redecide again and again how much hurt you can take and when you have to leave the doing good for the sake of keeping yourself whole."

Learn From Those You Help

Even with all the stress and obstacles we face, one helper would not trade what she does for anything else, mostly because of the opportunities she feels to continually learn and grow.

"Learn from your clients," she says. "They are the best books you can read, the most tasty morsel you can savor. Respect them as your teachers, laugh with them like you will with your pilgrims. At the same time, know yourself well. Do any work necessary to keep life in perspective."

Take Risks

"Don't rely too much on the personal responses of people that you help. You become too dependent upon their feedback. Yes, I've noted the contradition. So when you feel you are doing the right thing based upon your professional and ethical judgment, go ahead. Don't be afraid to offend some people in the process of helping. It might be what makes the difference. Thus don't be a people pleaser."

There are differences, of course, between the risks that an experienced practitioner can take based on years of experience and the gut instincts of a beginner who is first starting out. Your first responsibility is always, if you can't help someone, to at least do no harm.

Believe in Yourself

"In order to make a difference, you have to believe you can make a difference." A nursing supervisor reminds herself of this point when she has her doubts. "Lots of times I just don't know if what I did was helpful or not. When I start thinking this way, it's hard to keep going. Later I find out that the patient I was working with, or the nurse I was mentoring, really did feel grateful. You just don't know."

Practice What You Preach

One of the best parts of helping is not only what you can do for others, but what you can do for yourself. You would be silly, if not downright negligent, to encourage others to do things that you are not willing to do in your own life.

"Be proud of who you are," advises the Mäori mediator you met earlier. "Know your *whakapapa* [ancestral family tree]. Show *wehi* [humility], *aroha* [love], *ihi* [excellence], *manaki* [care] in all that you do. Enter into the field because you would like to assist and support people in conflict rather than patronize people. So do it for the right reasons. Seek the assistance and skills of people who are experienced and want to help you. Be willing to learn. Look at people from within a wide cultural context rather than from your own. Be prepared to be 'knocked about,' both personally and culturally. Learn from all that you encounter."

On Virtue

A retired teacher is at first skeptical that anything she could offer would be all that useful. "I don't think there is anything I could *tell* someone that would matter. I don't have any advice. What I would urge instead is that beginners should keep the fire burning within them. Talk about this stuff to anyone who will listen. Spend time around other people who have in them what you want for yourself. All I can do is be a cheerleader for others who are starting out."

We are back to passion again. We do good not through a single act but through a lifetime of commitment, living in accordance with those virtues and ideals we hold most dear. In describing what it means to be a "virtuous" helper, Cohen and Cohen (1999) say that such a standard of morality means that you do good, not because of any ulterior motive, or even because such behavior was called for in a given situation, but because it is intrinsically right. Such a helper, they write, "would seek to be honest with her clients not merely because this behavior is itself a way toward the goal of maximizing profit (supposing that 'morality pays' by attracting clients) but because honesty itself is to be valued" (pp. 19–20).

☐ How to Encourage More Help-Giving in Others

A number of authors have suggested things we might do to make the world a more giving, generous, and compassionate place (Hunt, 1990; P. M. Oliner & Oliner, 1995; Rosenman, 1999).

- Feel privileged and grateful for what others have done for you; pass it on.
- Confront your own hypocrisy.
- Practice more what you preach to others.
- Follow the lead of Jesus, Mohammed, Buddha, Moses, Brigham Young, Gandhi, and other religious leaders. Walk in their footsteps.
- Teach values and a higher state of morality that emphasizes collective responsibility for everyone's welfare.
- Redefine status as coming not from possessions or material worth but from acts of goodness.
- Reflect on what gives meaning to your life.
- Practice love and empathy wherever and whenever you can.

Most of all, be virtuous. Virtue is the attribute that represents the highest ideal of what is good in human nature. It is the highest standard of conduct and has several distinct features (Jeffries, 1998):

1. *Temperance.* Restraint, patience, moderation, self-control, and modesty allow one to preserve energy and set limits on what is possible,
2. *Fortitude.* Internal strength in the face of adversity, stability, perseverance, overcoming reluctance and fears, taking risks,
3. *Justice.* Equality, fairness, what is right and just,

4. *Charity*. Benevolence, mercy, forgiveness, empathy, generosity,
5. *Prudence*. Sound choices, commands the other virtues to act effectively.

Move Beyond Self

Kohn (1990) believes that egoism and self-absorption are the greatest obstacles that get in the way of helping. We live in a culture that prizes individualism. There is a national obsession with self-esteem, self-concept, self-confidence, self-determination, self, self, self. Everything is about *me*, what *I* want, what makes *me* happy. This narcissism and intense self involvement is obviously an impediment to greater concern for others.

Helping is mostly about getting outside of your "self," in order to connect fully with another.

Confronting Racism

Racism results from one group of people making judgments about others who are "not like us." When one particular group controls resources and opportunities, which is the case in almost every human and animal society, the "have-nots" are made to suffer. Racism is almost always "faceless," Gladding (1999) points out. It is the result of misunderstanding and mistrust. Once people are known as individuals, there often develops a common bond. This is something that must not only be thought about and talked about, but acted upon.

Giving lip service to multiculturalism and ethnic diversity is, of course, politically correct. Being opposed to racism, sexism, and other forms of oppression are also popular positions to take, both within helping professions and in society at large. The problem is that we talk a good game but don't act on what we say we believe.

Almost nobody you know will admit to being a racist, or even being biased (which is really ridiculous since a bias is a preference for something or against something). Yet who are your neighbors? Who have been your lovers? Who are your best friends? Just how much diversity do you have among your most intimate confidantes?

There is no shame in liking to be around people who are "like us." Who wouldn't prefer to be around others who share their interests, values, and priorities? Certainly it is also stimulating to be around people who hold alternative views, but it can also be extremely threatening and frustrating.

So, back to the primary question: What do you actually *do* to attack racism and oppression around you and in your community? What have you done in the past to feed the starving, find shelter for the homeless, and provide care for the needy? Regardless of your efforts in the past, the answer is not nearly enough.

The last thing in the world you need from me is another lecture or sermon about the merits of service. We have enough token gestures from people who make charitable donations for tax deductions and a ticket to heaven. We need a lot more people who reach out to others not because they will get brownie points on God's ledger, or because they enjoy others' approval, but purely for the intrinsic joy of giving.

Let the Experiences Inside You

Upon reflecting on the time he spent living and working in the slums of Calcutta with the most deprived people on earth, Lapierre (1985) reports that he was profoundly changed by the experience. "Living with the inhabitants of the City of Joy completely transformed my sense of priorities and my assessment of the true values of life" (p. 510). How upsetting can a rude clerk, rush-hour traffic, or career disappointment be when you've seen people all around you struggling to find enough food to eat?

Random Acts of Kindness

Give something to someone you don't know every day. I don't mean your money or clothes necessarily, but the gift of your compassion, your attention, your smile, your benevolence, your patience. Extend a part of yourself without expecting or wanting anything in return.

Read Inspirational Memoirs or Biographies

Study the lives of those who have devoted their lives to service. Read biographies about the likes of Mahatma Ghandi, Florence Nightingale, Mother Theresa, Albert Schweitzer, or Lawrence of Arabia. For starters, read Lapierre's (1985) *The City of Joy*, Ram Das and Gorman's (1985) *How Can I Help?*, Keneally's (1983) *Schindler's List*, Brehony's (1999) *Ordinary Grace*.

Promote Other-Oriented Values in Organizations

Korsgaard, Meglino, and Lester (1997) advocated a movement away from self-interest in organizations to emphasize a spirit of cooperation, mutuality, and teamwork. In several studies, they found that employees with the highest concern for others did not conform to the usual predictions for maximizing their own self-interest. Instead, they were often inclined to put their own needs and potential gains aside for the sake of others.

Since many organizations work on a merit system in which employees are rewarded for their individual performance when compared to peers, this competition discourages altruistic and other-oriented values in lieu of selfish motives. In many universities, for example, professors are rank-ordered in terms of their research productivity, the highest raises going to those first on the list. Such an incentive program not only dampens intrinsically based motivation (those who write for the love of the activity), but it discourages faculty from working cooperatively.

Other organizational cultures, notably in Asia, stress a far more cooperative, other-based value system in which individual achievement is considerably less important than meeting group objectives. This actually parallels behavioral patterns in the animal kingdom in which the prosperity of any member or a troop, pack, or herd is largely dependent on how successful the group is.

There are many organizations, as well as churches, synagogues, and countless community agencies, that are devoted to serving others. If you are not already working in such a setting, you may wish to contact an organization to broaden your helping experience. Some of the more well-known groups include:

Vista
1201 New York Avenue, NW
Washington, DC 20525
    Volunteers in Service to America provides stipends and living allowances for work in poor and disadvantaged areas.

• • •

Peace Corp
1990 K Street, NW
Washington, DC 20526
    This federal agency promotes world peace and mutual understanding by sending volunteers to needy areas in order to provide assistance, consultation, expertise, and support. Projects often focus on small business development, agriculture, health, education, and development.

• • •

Big Brothers, Big Sisters
230 North 13th Street
Philadelphia, PA 19107
bbbsa@aol.com

Matches children from single-parent homes with adult role models. Volunteers act as mentors in order to provide guidance and support.

• • •

Habitat For Humanity
121 Habitat Street
Americus, GA 31709
public_info@habitat.org
   Volunteers build housing in partnership with local communities.

• • •

Action Without Borders
www.idealist.org
   This agency maintains a web site that acts as a clearinghouse for hundreds of volunteer organizations that provide volunteer and internship experiences, as well as job openings with nonprofit groups.

• • •

Fourth World Movement
7600 Willow Hill Drive
Landover, MD 20785
fourworl@his.com
   Volunteers work in literacy, libraries, and computer projects for most impoverished areas of the world.

• • •

American Red Cross
8111 Gatehouse Drive
Falls Church, VA 22042
   Huge network of assistance programs are geared towards disaster relief and armed forces.

   This is just the tiniest sample of possibilities. Most local newspapers list volunteer opportunities each week and various resources in the local library will have suggestions as well.

☐ Change the World, or Your Small Part of It

Every night before I go to sleep, I ask myself what I have done during the day that was useful or helpful to someone else. Sometimes it might be something apparently inconsequential: a warm smile to the bank teller or a compliment to the phone solicitor. Other times it feels like I single-handedly saved the world through a caring gesture.

You have decided to be a helper because you feel the calling. You feel the passion and commitment to service. With considerable training, supervision, and experience, you *can* make a huge difference in the lives that you touch. It all begins with the acts of good that you do every day, the gestures of compassion and caring that define your existence and give meaning to your life—that which makes you a helper.

REFERENCES

Adler, A. (1956). *The individual psychology of Alfred Adler* (H. L. Ansbacher & R. R. Ansbacher, Eds.). New York: Norton.

Adler, A. (1979). *Superiority and social interest* (H. L. Ansbacher & R. R. Ansbacher, Eds.). New York: Norton.

Ashton, M. C., Paunonen, S. V., Helmes, E., & Jackson, D. N. (1998). Kin altruism, reciprocal altruism, and big five personality factors. *Evolution and Human Behavior, 19*, 243–255.

Batson, C. D. (1986). Where is the altruism in the altruistic personality? *Journal of Personality and Social Psychology, 50*, 212–220.

Beck, J. S. (1995). *Cognitive therapy: Basics and beyond.* New York: Guilford.

Belson, R. (1992, September/October). Ten tried-and-true methods to achieve therapist burnout. *Family Therapy Networker, 22.*

Bemak, F., & Epp, L. (1996). The 12th curative factor: Love as an agent of healing in group psychotherapy. *Journal For Specialists in Group Work, 21*(2), 118–127.

Bierhoff, H. W., Kiein, R., & Kramp, P. (1991). Evidence for the altruistic personality from data on accident research. *Journal of Personality, 59*, 263–280.

Bluffer-Hrdy, S. (1976). Care and exploitation of non-human primate infants by conspecifics other than the mother. *Advances in the Study of Behavior, 6*, 101–158.

Bohart, A., & Tallman, K. (1999). *How clients make therapy work: The process of active self-healing.* Washington, D.C.: American Psychological Association.

Breggin, P. R. (1997). *The heart of being helpful: Empathy and the creation of a healing presence.* New York: Springer-Verlag.

Brehony, K. A. (1999). *Ordinary grace: An examination of the roots of compassion, altruism, and empathy, and the ordinary individuals who help others in extraordinary ways.* Riverhead Books.

Bremner, R. H. (1994). *Giving: Charity and philanthropy in history.* New Brunswick, NJ: Transaction Publishers.

Breuer, G. (1982). *Sociobiology and the human dimension.* Cambridge, England: Cambridge University Press.

Brothers, L. (1989). A biological perspective on empathy. *American Journal of Psychiatry, 146,* 16.

Buss, D. M. (1999). *Evolutionary psychology: The new science of the mind.* Boston: Allyn and Bacon.

Carbonell, J. L., & Figley, C. R. (1996). When trauma hits home: Personal trauma and the family therapist. *Journal of Marital and Family Therapy, 22*, 53–58.

Cohen, E. D., & Cohen, G. S. (1999). *The virtuous therapist.* Belmont, CA: Wadsworth.

Connelly, J. (1998). *Bringing out the dead.* New York: Knopf.

Corey, M. S., & Corey, G. (1998). *Becoming a helper* (3rd ed.). Pacific Grove, CA: Brooks/Cole.

Csikszentmihalyi, M. (1975). *Beyond boredom and anxiety.* San Franciso: Jossey-Bass.

Csikszentmihalyi, M. (1999). If we are so rich, why aren't we happy? *American Psychologist, 10,* 821–827.

Curtis, R. C., & Stricker, G. (Eds.). (1991). *How people change: Inside and outside therapy.* New York: Plenum.

Daly, M., & Wilson, M. (1988). *Homicide.* Hawthorne, NY: Aldine.

Darwin, C. (1859/1964). *On the origin of species.* Cambridge, MA: Harvard University Press.

De la Bruyere, J. (1688/1993). Characters. *Columbia Dictionary of Quotations.* New York: Columbia University Press.

Doherty, W. J. (1995). *Soul searching.* New York: Basic Books.

Dugatkin, L. (1999). *Cheating monkeys and citizen bees: The nature of cooperation in animals and humans.* New York: The Free Press.

Eisenberg, N. (1982). *The development of prosocial behavior.* New York: Academic Press.

Ellis, A. (1995). *Better, deeper, and more enduring brief therapy: The rational emotive behavior therapy approach.* New York: Brunner/Mazel.

Fellner, C. H., & Marshall, J. R. (1981). Kidney donors revisited. In J. P. Rushton & R. M. Sorrentino (Eds.), *Altruism and helping behavior.* Hillsdale, NJ: Erlbaum.

Figley, C. R. (1995). Compassion fatigue: Toward a new understanding of the costs of caring. In B. H. Stamm (Ed.), *Secondary Traumatic Stress.* Lutherville, MD: Sidran Press.

Fish, J. (1973). *Placebo therapy.* San Francisco: Jossey-Bass.

Frank, J. (1961). *Persuasion and healing.* New York: Schocken.

Freudenberger, H. J. (1975). The staff burn-out syndrome in alternative institutions. *Psychotherapy, 12,* 73–82.

Galston, W. A. (1993). Cosmopolitan altruism. In E. Paul, F. Miller, & J. Paul (Eds.), *Altruism.* New York: Cambridge University Press.

Gladding, S. (1999). The faceless nature of racism: A counselor's journey. *Journal of Humanistic Education and Development, 37*(3), 182–187.

Glantz, K., & Pearce, J. K. (1989). *Exiles from eden: Psychotherapy from an evolutionary perspective.* New York: Norton.

Gould, J. L., & Marler, P. (1987, January). Learning by instinct. *Scientific American,* 74–85.

Guy, J. D. (1987). *The personal life of the psychotherapist.* New York: Wiley.

Guy, J. D., Poelstra, P. L., & Stark, M. J. (1987). Personal distress and therapeutic effectiveness. *Professional Psychology: Research and Practice, 20,* 18–50.

Haldane, J. B. S. (1955). Population genetics. *New Biology, 18,* 34–51.

Hoffman, M. L. (1981). The development of empathy. In J. P. Rushton & R. M. Sorrentino (eds.), *Altruism and helping behavior.* Hillsdale, NJ: Erlbaum.

Hoffman, M. L. (1990). Empathy and justice motivation. *Motivation and Emotion, 14,* 151–172.

Hovarth, A. O., & Symonds, B. D. (1991). Relation between working alliance and outcome in psychotherapy: A meta-analysis. *Journal of Counseling Psychology, 38,* 139–149.

Howard, J. A. (1975). *The flesh-colored cage.* New York: Hawthorn.

Hubble, M. A., Duncan, B. L., & Miller, S. D. (1999). *Heart and soul of change.* Washington, DC: American Psychological Association.

Hunt, M. (1990). *The compassionate beast: What science is discovering about the humane side of humankind.* New York: William Morrow.

Independent Sector. (1996). *Giving and volunteering in the United States: Findings from a national survey.* Washington, DC: Author.

Jeffries, V. (1998). Virtue and altruistic personality. *Sociological Perspectives, 41,* 151–166.

Jennings, L., & Skovholt, T. M. (1999). The cognitive, emotional, and relational characteristics of master therapists. *Journal of Counseling Psychology, 46*(1), 3–11.

Kalb, C., & Rogers, A. (1999, June 14). Stress. *Newsweek,* 56–63.

Kanfer, F. H., & Goldstein, A. P. (Eds.). (1986). *Helping people change* (3rd ed.). New York: Pergamon.

Keneally, T. (1983). *Schindler's list.* New York: Penguin Books.

Kissinger, H. A. (1999, May 31). *New world disorder. Newsweek,* 41–43.

Kohn, A. (1990). *The brigher side of human nature: Altruism and empathy in everyday life.* New York: Basic Books.

Korsgaard, M. A., Beglino, B. M., & Lester, S. W. (1997). Beyond helping: Do other-oriented values have broader implications in organizations? *Journal of Applied Psychology, 82,* 160–177.

Kottler, J. A. (1991). *The compleat therapist.* San Francisco: Jossey-Bass.

Kottler, J. A. (1992). *Compassionate therapy: Working with difficult clients.* San Francisco: Jossey-Bass.

Kottler, J. A. (1993). *On being a therapist.* San Francisco: Jossey-Bass.

Kottler, J. A. (Ed.). (1996a). *Finding your way as a counselor.* Alexandria, VA: American Counseling Association.

Kottler, J. A. (1996b). *The language of tears.* San Francisco: Jossey-Bass.

Kottler, J. A. (1999). *The therapist's workbook: Self-assessment, self-care, and self-improvement exercises for mental health professionals.* San Francisco: Jossey-Bass.

Kottler, J. A. (in press). *Making changes last.* Philadelphia: Brunner/Routledge.

Kottler, J. A.. & Brown, R. W. (2000). *Introduction to therapeutic counseling.* Pacific Grove, CA: Brooks/Cole.

Kottler, J. A., & Hazler, R. (1997). *What you never learned in graduate school.* New York: Norton.

Kottler, J. A., Sexton, T., & Whiston, S. (1994). *The heart of healing: Relationships in therapy.* San Francisco: Jossey-Bass.

Kottler, J., & Zehm, S. (2000). *On being a teacher: The human dimension* (2nd ed.). Newbury Park, CA: Corwin Press.

Lapierre, D. (1985). *The city of joy.* New York: Warner Books.

Latané, B. (1981). The psychology of social impact. *American Psychologist, 36,* 343–356.

Latané, B., & Darley, J. M. (1970). *The unresponsive bystander: Why doesn't anyone help?* New York: Appleton-Century-Crofts.

Luks, A. (1988, October). Helper's high. *Psychology Today,* 39–42.

Mahoney, M. J. (1991). *Human change processes.* New York: Wiley.

Maslach, C. (1982). *Burnout: The cost of caring.* Englewood Cliffs, NJ: Prentice-Hall.

Maslow, A. (1970). *Motivation and personality.* New York: Harper & Row.

Masson, J. M., & McCarthy, S. (1995). *When elephants weep.* New York: Delacorte.

Miller, L. (1993). Who are the best psychotherapists? *Psychotherapy in Private Practice, 12,* 1–18.

Monroe, K. (1991). John Donne's people: Explaining differences between rational actors and altruists through cognitive frameworks. *Journal of Politics, 53*(2), 394–433.

Monroe, K. (1996). *The heart of altruism: Perceptions of a common humanity.* Princeton, NJ: Princeton University Press.

Moore, T. (1994). *Soul mates: Honoring the mysteries of love and relationship.* New York: Harper-Collins.

Oliner, P. M., & Oliner, S. P. (1995). *Toward a caring society: Ideas into action.* Westport, CT: Praeger.

Oliner, S. P., & Oliner, P. M. (1988). *The altruistic personality: Rescuers of Jews from Nazi Europe.* New York: Free Press.

Orlinsky, D. E., & Howard, K. I. (1986). Process and outcome in psychotherapy. In S. L. Garfield & A. E. Bergin (Eds.), *Handbook of psychotherapy and behavior change.* New York: Wiley.

Pearlman, L. A. (1995). Self-care for trauma therapists: Ameliorating vicarious traumatization. In B. H. Stamm (Ed.), *Secondary traumatic stress.* Lutherville, MD: Sidran Press.

Pearlman, L. A., & Saakvitne, K. W. (1995). *Trauma and the therapists: Countertransference and vicarious traumatization in psychotherapy with incest survivors.* New York: Norton.

Piliavin, J. A., & Charng, H. W. (1990). Altruism: A review of recent theory and research. *Annual Review of Sociology, 16,* 27–65.

Prochaska, J. O., Di Clemente, C. C., & Norcross, J. L. (1992). In search of how people change. *American Psychologist, 47,* 1102–1114.

Ram Das, & Bush, M. (1992). *Compassion in action.* New York: Bell Tower.

Ram Das, & Gorman, P. (1985). *How can I help? Stories and reflections on service.* New York: Knopf.

Rissing, S., Pollock, G., Higgins, M., Hagen, R., & Smith, D. (1989). Foraging specialization with relatedness or dominance about co-founding ant queens. *Nature, 338,* 420–422.

Rogers, C. R. (1961). *On becoming a person.* Boston: Houghton Mifflin.

Rosenbloom, D. J., Pratt, A. C., & Pearlman, L. A. (1995). Helpers' responses to trauma work: Understanding and intervening in an organization. In B. H. Stamm (Ed.), *Secondary traumatic stress.* Lutherville, MD: Sidran Press.

Rosenman, S. (1999). Compassionate heroes, bystanders, and the reformation of society. *Journal of Psychohistory, 26*(2), 611–624.

Rushton, J. P. (1976). Socializiation and the altruistic behavior of children. *Psychological Bulletin, 83,* 898–913.

Rushton, J. P. (1981). The altruistic personality. In J. P. Rushton & R. M. Sorrentino (Eds.), *Altruism and helping behavior.* Hillsdale, NJ: Erlbaum.

Sarason, S. (1995). *Caring and compassion in clinical practice.* Northvale, NJ: Jason Aronson.

Schroeder, D. A., Penner, L. A., Dovidio, J. F., & Piliavin, J. A. (1995). *The psychology of helping and altruism: Problems and puzzles.* New York: McGraw-Hill.

Sherman, P. W. (1980). The meaning of nepotism. *American Naturalist, 116,* 604–606.

Singer, P. (1981). *The expanding circle: Ethics and sociobiology.* New York: New American Library.

Snyder, M., Omoto, A. E., & Crain, A. L. (1999). Punished for their good deeds: Stigmatization of AIDS volunteers. *American Behavioral Scientist, 42,* 1175–1192.

Sober, E., & Wilson, D. S. (1998). *Unto others: The evolution and psychology of unselfish behavior.* Cambridge, MA: Harvard University Press.

Sussman, M. E. (Ed.). (1995). *A perilous calling: The hazards of psychotherapy practice.* New York: Wiley.

Thomas, L. (1974). *Lives of a cell.* New York: Viking.

Thomas, L. (1979). *The medusa and the snail.* New York: Viking.

Thomas, L. (1983). *Late night thoughts on listening to Mahler's ninth symphony.* New York: Viking Press.

Trivers, R. L. (1971). The evolution of reciprocal altruism. *Quarterly Review of Biology, 46,* 35–57.

Van Hesteren, F. (1992). The self in moral agency: Toward a theoretical model of the ideal altruistic personality. In P. M. Oliner et al. (Eds.), *Embracing the other.* New York: University Press.

Watts, R. E. (1999). The vision of Adler: An introduction. In R. E. Watts & J. Carlson (Eds.), *Interventions and strategies in counseling and psychotherapy.* Philadelphia: Accelerated Development.

Wenegrat, B. (1984). *Sociobiology and mental disorder.* Reading, MA: Addison-Wesley.

White, G. D. (1998). Trauma treatment training for Bosnian and Croatian mental health workers. *American Journal of Orthopsychiatry, 68,* 58–62.

Williams, A. B., Haber, D., Weaver, G. D., & Freeman, J. L. (1998). Altruistic activity: Does it make a difference in the senior center?, *International Journal of Aging and Human Development, 22,* 31–39.

Williams, M. B., & Sommer, J. F. (1995). Self-care and the vulnerable therapist. In B. H. Stamm (Ed.), *Secondary traumatic stress.* Lutherville, MD: Sidran Press.

Wilson, E. O. (1975). *Sociobiology: The new synthesis.* Cambridge, MA: Harvard University Press.

Wilson, E. O. (1979). *On human nature.* New York: Bantam.

Wilson, J. P., & Lindy, J. D. (1994). *Countertransference in the treatment of PTSD.* New York: Guilford.

Wright, R. (1994). *The moral animal.* New York: Pantheon.

Yassen, J. (1995). Preventing secondary compassion fatigue. In C. R. Figley (Ed.), *Compassion fatigue.* New York: Brunner/Mazel.

Zahn-Waxler, C. (1983). Early altruism and guilt. *Academic Psychological Bulletin, 5,* 247–259.

Zahn-Waxler, C., Radke-Yarrow, M., Wagner, E., & Chapman, M. (1992). *Development of concern for others. Developmental Psychology, 28,* 126–136.

ABOUT THE AUTHOR

Jeffrey Kottler is one of the most prolific authors in the helping professions. He has authored a dozen texts for counselors, teachers, and therapists (*Introduction to Therapeutic Counseling*, 4th Ed., *Advanced Group Leadership*, 2nd Ed., *Nuts and Bolts of Helping*, *Counseling Skills for Teachers*, 2nd Ed.) and another dozen books on the nature of change (*On Being a Therapist; What You Never Learned in Graduate School; Growing a Therapist*) and on teaching (*On Being a Teacher; Classrooms Under the Influence; Succeeding With Difficult Students*). He has also authored several trade books that describe rather complex phenomena in highly accessible prose (*Travel That Can Change Your Life; Private Moments, Secret Selves; The Language of Tears*). Finally, he has dealt with very provocative, sensitive subjects in a style that is both engaging and dignified in the *New York Times* bestseller *The Last Victim: Inside the Minds of Serial Killers*.

Jeffrey has been an educator for 25 years. He has worked as a teacher, counselor, and therapist in preschools, middle schools, mental health centers, crisis centers, universities, community colleges, and private practice. He has served as a Fulbright Scholar and Senior Lecturer in Peru (1980) and Iceland (2000), as well as worked in dozens of countries as a consultant and trainer specializing in multicultural issues.

Jeffrey is currently a faculty member at the University of New England in Armidale, Australia and Hong Kong. He lives in Las Vegas, Nevada.

INDEX